LAO TZU

TAO
TE
CHING

Translated by Ralph Alan Dale

Photographs by John Cleare

WATKINS
Sharing Wisdom Since
1893

To Lao Tzu who, through his courage, imagination, intuition, insight and wisdom, conceived of the Great Integrity (Tao).

To the millions of tribal people who lived in the Great Integrity, thereby proving to us that it is as natural to our species just as it is, and always has been, the only way of life ever known to every other species.

To the hundreds of millions of human beings who have been victimized by our loss of the Great Integrity during the era we euphemistically call civilization, and to the countless species that were sacrificed at the altars of our civilizations.

To the astonishing technologies that civilizations created as bi-products of scarcity relative to need, and whose *modus vivendi* was and still continues to be greed. But these technologies have taken such qualitative leaps that now, paradoxically, they have become fundamental to our potential to realize planetary abundance, and so the means to 'anachronize' the very system of greed that originally generated them.

To the hundreds of thousands of courageous visionaries who have dedicated their lives to the rebirth of the Great Integrity during the myriad centuries when, at most, it could enlighten our hearts and dreams, but could not yet be achieved as an alternative way of life.

To the tens of millions of us who today are joining hands across the planet, committed to the conscious evolution of the Great Integrity Renaissance, whose time has finally come.

To the billions of future human beings who will live the Great Integrity in dimensions far beyond our wildest dreams, and who will forever be appreciative of Lao Tzu, of the tribal people, of civilizations' victims, of our ultimate technologies, of the courageous visionaries, and of those of us who today are so fortunate to be the midwives of the Great Transformation.

And to my wife, Hendrina. Our unconditional love has fueled my personal inspiration to write this book, piercing years of armoring, and opening my heart to the Great Integrity.

Tao Te Ching
Ralph Alan Dale

This edition published in the UK and USA in 2016 by Watkins, an imprint of Watkins Media Limited
19 Cecil Court
London WC2N 4EZ

enquiries@watkinspublishing.com

Copyright © Watkins Media Limited 2016
Text copyright © Watkins Media Limited 2002, 2016
Photography copyright © John Cleare 2002, 2016

The right of Ralph Alan Dale to be identified as the Author of this text has been asserted in accordance with the Copyright, Designs and Patents Act of 1988.

Designed and typeset by Clare Thorpe

A CIP record for this book is available from the British Library

ISBN: 978-1-78028-964-9

10 9 8 7 6 5 4 3 2 1

Typeset in Adobe Garamond
Printed in China
www.watkinspublishing.com

CONTENTS

FOREWORD

By Barbara Marx Hubbard

Author and President of the Foundation for Conscious Education

The spiral of our evolutionary progress is turning back in time to reconnect with the great sage Lao Tzu. In his understanding of the Tao, we find vital guidance and a natural way for us to realign with the implicate enfolded order in evolution. He stands before us, a beneficent presence, gently reminding us to become aware of transformational patterns and to practice conscious evolution.

The Great Integrity is his beautiful description of the whole connected field of de-ideologized reality out of which our liberating alternatives are arising. He is a post-post-modern teacher, standing beyond the artificial constructions and deconstructions of current thought, serving as our guardian and guide of the perennial wisdom of humanity. He calls to us to re-enter the harmony of nature, now as sovereign whole persons. No longer children seeking external deities, or self-centered materialists seeking power over nature and each other, we become co-creators with the great creating process itself, integral active agents of the Great Integrity.

About 2,000 years before Lao Tzu's time, the momentous transition took place from the earlier phase of human history – when we lived in relative harmony with nature, caring for each other by necessity – to the coercive civilizations of the past 5,000 years. At this transformational point, agriculture gave us the capacity to create a surplus by forcing the majority to enrich a minority which usurped the power to control society. The egalitarian social structures of the far longer human past were shattered. It was no longer a biological necessity to care for each other. Rather, there was an advantage for some to gain superiority over others. We moved, in Riane Eisler's phrase, from a partnership model to a dominator model. Masters and slaves, wealthy and poor, armies and weapons of mass destruction developed. However, the benefits of this last phase were surely great, culminating in science, individuality and – for some – freedom, abundance and education. None the less, in our time, the dysfunctional ties of this form of social structure have now become apparent.

If we continue, even one more generation, over-populating, polluting, warring and ever widening the gap between the rich and the poor, we see the evolutionary "handwriting on the wall". We can destroy our life-support systems and even make our species extinct.

As Einstein said, we cannot solve our problems in the same state of consciousness in which we created them. The ancient teaching of Lao Tzu now becomes the new necessity. Modern evolutionary thinkers, writers and activists are seeking to reconnect with the patterns in natural systems, beginning to learn how to become co-evolutionary with these patterns which Lao Tzu called the *Tao* and which Dr. Dale translates as the *Great Integrity*.

Lao Tzu is a masterful guide, and Ralph Alan Dale has given us the precise interpretation that we need so that we may apply this teaching to our vital quest for co-evolution and co-creation. Lao Tzu's time has come, and this book is a magnificent, clear, poetic rendering of the ancient truth now reborn in our age. It is as if Lao Tzu himself has guided the understanding of Dr. Dale, whose reverence and brilliance shine through every word.

INTRODUCTION

OUR FASCINATION WITH THE TAO TE CHING

The *Tao Te Ching*[1] is an ancient Chinese book composed of only 5,000 characters and written perhaps as early as the 6th century BCE,[2] by Lao Tzu, the legendary father of Taoism.

For centuries, this small book of Lao Tzu's sayings had no name. It was like the Tao itself that is introduced right at the outset:

> *The Tao that can be told*
> *is not the universal Tao.*
> *The name that can be named*
> *is not the universal name.*[3]

More than four centuries after Lao Tzu was supposed to have lived, Si-Ma Qian (Ssu-Ma Ch'ien) observed that the book was divided into two parts. Thereafter people began to refer to these two parts as *Tao* and *Te*. Still later, the book was divided into 81 sections. Verses 1–37 are called the *Tao* section because Verse 1 begins with the word, *Tao*. Verses 38–81 are called the *Te* section because Verse 38 begins with the word *Te*. Then the word *Ching* was added to the title. Ching means *ancient text* or *classic*.

Tao means *path*. For Lao Tzu, it signifies not just any path, but the specific path to living in concordance with the unity of the universe. According to Lao Tzu, it is the nature of nature to issue from an inextricable relationship of every part to the whole. To live life in accord with the Tao is to be in harmony with all others, with the environment and with one's self. It is to live in synchronicity with processes, and to be completely authentic, sincere, natural and innocent. The word *integrity* embraces all these characteristics. Tao also implies the inexhaustible greatness and wonderfulness of the universe and every part of it.[4] All these propositions provide what modern science would call a theory of the nature of the universe. I therefore translate Tao as the *theory of the Great Integrity*. Te means *virtue* or the practice of the Tao, and Ching, as already indicated above, means a *classic book* or *guide*. I therefore translate the *Tao Te Ching* as *a guide to the theory and practice of the Great Integrity*.

The *Tao Te Ching* is one of the most widely translated books in the world. During the past 2,400 years there may have been as many as 1,400 different interpretations, with perhaps 700 extant.[5] This book continues to fascinate people throughout the world. Why?

I believe it is because the *Tao Te Ching* confronts and offers an alternative to our schizoid ways of thinking, feeling and behaving. Every section appeals to an innate holistic wisdom that our innermost being has longed for during all these past so-called civilized millennia – sometimes consciously, often unconsciously.

Lao Tzu's words invite us to transcend words since words are used as the rationalizations of the tyrannies that we have established over each other.[6] He offers us what in his time were alternative Utopian pathways to a more harmonious life. Today, in this 21st century, the Great Integrity presents itself as a practical and achievable goal and perhaps as the only alternative to the extinction of our own species.

THE PARADOX OF LANGUAGE

Right at the beginning, Lao Tzu invites us to transcend words:

> *In the infancy of the universe,*
> *there were no names.*
> *Naming fragments the mysteries of life*
> *into ten thousand things and their manifestations.*[7]

But how does one take issue with the world of words without using words? By being rather than by arguing. That, in fact, was Lao Tzu's way. He probably never wrote this book, because polemics was the very target of his advocacy.[8] More likely, many generations of his disciples and followers summarized his philosophy of life in these metaphoric fragments which sing the literary music of the right brain,[9] the transcendence of language through unordinary language.

Because paradox is the principal mode of Lao Tzu's thought processes, and because it is the nature of the Chinese language, especially ancient Chinese, to be poetic, I have rendered these 81 sections as verses, although the original is written more like Chinese prose than poetry. Moreover, how else than through poetry can one employ the left brain to transcend itself? How else can one criticize logical thinking without using logic? And how else does one merge yin and yang[10] whose very nature expresses polarization?

It is the paradox of every poet to have to transcend the logical function of language through language. It is a higher level of paradox when the very content of the poetry is dedicated to this transcendence. The ultimate consistency of Lao Tzu's wisdom is for us to communicate through silence, but consistency is also a negation of his wisdom. Since the *Tao Te Ching* itself is a communication through words, the very act of writing or reading this book is an affirmation that words are not really the enemy. The enemy is the perversion of words to manipulate the disadvantaged, and their further perversion to rationalize the consequent inhumanities of these manipulations.[11] On the contrary, the words of Lao Tzu point us toward our liberation from inequities and injustices – that is, toward the Great Integrity.

TAO – THE GREAT INTEGRITY

What is the Tao? It is the oneness of all reality. According to Lao Tzu, the Tao or Great Integrity is the origin and nature of the Universe.[12] It is the way of life for all species on our planet, including human beings living in most tribal societies.

In ancient times
the people knew the Great Integrity
with subtlety and profundity.[13]

Later, since the advent of civilizations, we human beings lost the Great Integrity, exchanging our natural harmony with the universe for ego-oriented life styles. Paradoxically, Lao Tzu states that we will recover the Great Integrity without trying. So how is it possible for us to transform ourselves without trying to do so? There are two components of this paradox: The first is subjective and applies both to Lao Tzu's time as well as our own. The second is a unique objective aspect of our radical evolution in this 21st century.

(1) Lao Tzu doesn't mean by "not trying" that we should accept our present unhappy condition. He identifies trying with forcing. To act without trying means to act without coercion. He offers *being* as an alternative to *trying*. The implication is that even before we transform the world in accordance with our age-old dream,

we can transcend our indoctrination and life styles by being – or at least beginning to be – that totally human person that our species nature craves. Lao Tzu advises us to have the courage to begin to live in the future now as a means to our own transcendence.[14]

(2) This ability *to be* before we *become* is much more possible for us today than it was for people in Lao Tzu's time, because, in a sense, it is we, not Lao Tzu's contemporaries, who live in the evolutionary epoch of transition. Until now, in every civilization, relative economic scarcity has defined the objective conditions that have chained us to a way of life that violates our own natures as well as the nature of nature. But we 21st-century-ites have already discovered one of the fundamental prerequisites for the full actualization of our human species potentials by having created the technology to live in a planetary economy of abundance. The proviso, of course, is that we utilize this technology productively to fulfill the needs of all people on the planet instead of squandering it on intraspecies conflicts and gross inequitable distributions.

In fact, the contradiction between having achieved a qualitatively new level of technology and clinging anachronistically to our old social relations defines our main problem today. Instead of utilizing our new technological capacities to create a world of abundance, we turn into Frankensteins of mass destruction – vandalizing nature as well as our own material creations and ourselves. Indeed, we are already at the gates of technological liberation while our social, economic and political institutions and our spirituality live in a cultural limbo, oblivious that some of the main preconditions for our evolutionary transformation have already been achieved.

THE THREE ASPECTS OF LIBERATION

There is a developmental process through which we may become liberated from our limitations and distortions, and through which we can begin to enter the alternative world of the Great Integrity. We can identify three interdependent aspects: 1) Detoxifying the mental-emotional-spiritual garbage that we all inherit; 2) Returning to our own humanity; and 3) Transforming our institutions and ourselves to fully realize our human potential. These three aspects are metaphorically recounted in the following story.[15]

A few travelers were passing a Sufi monastery. Their curiosity led them to look through the open door to see what was happening. People were screaming, jumping, freaking out and, it seemed, just going completely mad. In the midst of all this chaos, the Master was sitting calmly and silently. The travelers said to each other that they thought that monasteries are where people go to attain enlightenment. However, here the Master seems to have attracted insanity. He also seems to be out of touch since he sits quietly meditating, apparently oblivious to the chaos going on all around him. The travelers left, shaking their heads in disbelief.

After a few months, these travelers once again came through that same town and passed the monastery. They again looked through the open door, expecting to see the raving maniacs. To their utter amazement, they observed the very same people, silently sitting in meditation. The contrast to their first observation seemed incomprehensible. Once again they left shaking their heads in disbelief.

A few months passed. Again these travelers returned to that town and, of course, were curious to see what was happening in the monastery. They tiptoed to the open door, and now found to their surprise that no one was screaming and no one was meditating. The entire monastery was empty. Only the Master was sitting there. This time their curiosity was so great that they entered the monastery and spoke with the Master.

"How is it," they asked, "that some time ago, when we first came upon this monastery, everybody was jumping around and shouting like they were insane? The second time we came, these same people were silently meditating. Now we have returned a third time, and no one is here. Can you explain this to us?"

"It is very simple," said the Master. "When you passed by the first time, the neophytes had just arrived and they were full of the world's madness, so I encouraged them to purge the 10,000 toxins that civilization distributes to everyone. The second time you came, they were exploring the quiet depths of their own innocence, their connections with the universe, their own human species natures. Now you have come when they have all returned to their homes because they are ready to allow their new consciousness to facilitate the transformation of their communities to more human ways of life. At this moment, I am awaiting the arrival of a new group of neophytes. When you pass by next time, there will again be madness."

THE GREAT INTEGRITY AND OUR ULTIMATE CHOICE

The life style of the Great Integrity, then, is not about withdrawal from civilization, nor about escaping into a life of meditation. It is about engagement with life. It is about commitment to transcending our inhumanity. It is about the process just described.

In other words, the Great Integrity is about a quiet revolution that (1) confronts the pathological yang (purging the old), (2) embraces the yin (entering the temple of our total humanity), and (3) liberates us individually and globally to function through our full species potential (the return of the enlightened ones to the community to be models of personal transformation and agents of social transformation). Lao Tzu's Great Integrity is nothing more nor less than the fulfillment of the potential that was given to us at the evolutionary birth of our species, a condition which took several million years to ripen. How unbelievably privileged we are to be the generations assigned the ultimate task: to be the midwives of our own rebirthing!

We are invited to enter the world of Lao Tzu neither as outsiders nor as insiders, neither as activists nor as "passivists", but as more than both. We are the generations of observer–facilitators of our own transformation and the transformation of the premises and institutions of all civilizations from ancient times to the present. These old premises and institutions are now not only contradictions of the Great Integrity, but life-threatening to all of us on this planet. Specifically, (1) they have increasingly subverted our very human nature, (2) they have caused thousands of species to become extinct, (3) they have now placed our own species on the endangered list, and (4) they have created the ultimate power to destroy all life on our planet.

We generations of human beings living today may have the awesome ultimate choice between total destruction – what John Somerville called *omnicide* – and total liberation – what Lao Tzu called the *Great Integrity*. We are invited to approach the Great Integrity as peaceful partisans, ready, willing and able to be the "transmogrifiers" for ourselves, for others, and for the planet. It is you and I who will write the final verses of the *Tao Te Ching*. With this reinvented book as one of our preludes and guides, we begin to prepare ourselves for a New Age of creativity, peace, abundance and planetary synergy.

We are invited to take the first steps in the creation of a world beyond beautiful and ugly, beyond rich and poor, advantaged and disadvantaged, beyond science

and religion, labor and profits, intelligent and stupid, left brain and right
brain, health and sickness, beyond all the painful dichotomies that civilizations
have created.

> *We know beauty because there is ugly.*
> *We know good because there is evil.*
> *Being and not being,*
> *having and not having,*
> *create each other.*[16]

How is it possible to transform our present personal and global malaise into the
Great Integrity? There are formidable obstacles:

(1) The extreme fragmentations that define our everyday lives, and that have been
inherited for more than 200 generations, function as ideological, emotional and
experiential entrapments.

(2) The only way of life we know, and that has been known by our parents and by
the parents of our parents, expresses the inhumanities and pathologies of a dying
social process. We have great difficulty imagining an alternative that has not been
widely experienced for thousands of years.

(3) We are programmed by our institutions to accept the miseries of our lives as
the only ones possible and desirable. Like the young child who remains dependent
and even devoted to the parents who brutalize her (because they are the only
parents and the only experience she knows), we tend to remain loyal to the very
political, economic and cultural institutions that threaten our health and our lives.

(4) Living in a world that often robs us of love, respect and beauty requires escapes
that easily become addictive. We are obligingly provided with a great variety:
television, films, alcohol, tobacco, various legal and illegal drugs, sexism, racism,
male chauvinism, national jingoism, religious sectarianism, addictive foods and
drinks, egoism, consumerism, neuroticism, psychoticism, sadism and masochism,
just to name a few.

(5) The lack of real political power by the vast majority, compared with the enormous power concentrated in the hands of the economic and political elite, creates the feeling of impotence that leads to the abdication of political responsibility and the cultivation of cynicism.

But these obstacles are not insurmountable. We have the power to transcend all these entrapments and to acquire a consciousness of the Great Integrity for an alternative way of life. One prerequisite is to be able to step back from our immediate experience and its paralyzing rationalizations.

Lao Tzu's ancient Chinese philosophy provides a window through which we can acquire such a perspective – one that can intellectually catapult us beyond the limitations and toxins of our everyday lives. This window invites us to view the entire evolution of our species in two phases characterized by the polarity that ancient Chinese philosophy calls Yin and Yang, while the resolution of this polarization clarifies our image of the Great Integrity.

THE EVOLUTION OF CONSCIOUSNESS AS SEEN THROUGH THE METAPHOR OF TWO AND ITS RESOLUTION IN THE GREAT INTEGRITY

Viewing the entire history of societies and of their corresponding forms of consciousness through the window of "two" reveals two enormous eras: 1) the *Yin Epoch* – more than two to five million years of hominid, horde, clan and tribal life characterized for the most part by communal living and expressing a Great Integrity consciousness and a predominance of right-cerebral hemispheric intuitive function, and 2) the *Yang Epoch* of the past few thousand years, defined by coercive civilizations, and by the predominance of the left cerebral hemisphere and its hegemony of analytical and alienated consciousness.[17] Lao Tzu in the 6th century BCE and we in the 21st century are part of this Yang Epoch.

Life today is an expression of the decline and fall of this second great phase, which accounts for the enormous social and individual trauma of our time. Although societies have come and gone in the past, there is a new ultimate danger that the current disintegration of civilization presents: the intolerable juxtaposition of extreme social pathology and high technology, a volatile mixture that can lead not only to the end of civilization, but also to the possibility of the very extinction of our species. *Speciescide*, and even the possibility of *omnicide*, is avoidable only if we are able to acquire a new consciousness and a third way of life, the very shapes of which were prophetically defined by Lao Tzu.

All of us living today (though we are not all aware of it) are transitional beings struggling (though sometimes counterproductively) to transcend the second epoch – life as fragmentations, sectarianisms and inhumanities – to enter into the Great Harmony of the Third Epoch.[18]

The transformations of our consciousness, our ways of being and our institutions require our understanding of and reactive participation in this evolutionary process. These transformations demand the emergence of an integral consciousness[19] and the unification of our left and right cerebral hemispheric functions.

What are the transitional forms of this consciousness through which we can begin to step into the Third Epoch?

(1) The gradual disengagement of our left cerebral cortex from its roles in effectuating and rationalizing our warfare against other human beings, against nature, and against our own essential selves, while further developing the analytical potentialities of this left brain disassociated from its coercive functions.

(2) The increasing engagement of our right cerebral cortex, the part of our consciousness that has been repressed by the hegemony of the left manipulating and rationalizing brain. Fortunately, civilizations have produced compensatory mechanisms, which can function as springboards for facilitating right-brain development; for example, the arts, spirituality, "altered" states of consciousness, holistic forms of science and medicine and the cultivation of intuitive and psychic abilities.

(3) Exploring the integration of left-brain analysis with right-brain intuition to evolve a new meta-scientific consciousness.

(4) Most important of all – the increasing experience of relating to the environ-ment, to each other and to ourselves through the Great Integrity – that is, through a re-humanization, reintegration, and re-harmonization that begins to transcend our Second Epoch habits, emotions and institutional forms of fragmentation.

LAO TZU AS THE SILENT PROPHET

Lao Tzu is said to have written the *Tao Te Ching*. However, as we have already pointed out, to have done so would, in itself, be a contradiction of the basic tenets of the book. According to the *Tao Te Ching*, life is to be experienced rather than philosophized.

> *The wise are heard*
> *through their silence,*
> *always self-full through selflessness.*[20]

Sensing this contradiction, one legend tells us that Lao Tzu was never interested in writing out his thoughts, but when he was leaving active life for the seclusion of the wilderness, he was stopped by a gatekeeper at the edge of civilization. This gatekeeper happened to have been one of his disciples. When Lao Tzu tried to pass through the gate, this disciple said to him: "If I let you pass, the world will be forever deprived of your wisdom, I will let you through only after you write out the principles by which you have led your life." The legend goes on to tell us that Lao Tzu, acceding to the urging and ultimatum of his disciple, wrote the *Tao Te Ching*, and passed through the gate to his reclusive retirement.

But the legend is an unlikely one, even more unlikely than those legends that claim the direct authorship of the books attributed to Sakyamuni, Confucius, Mencius and Chuang Tzu. Contrary to the legend, everything we know about Lao Tzu tells us that he makes no compromises, no bargains with the devil, not even when cajoled by the innocent demands of a well-meaning disciple. Moreover, whereas Confucius, Jesus, Mohammed, Buddha and Moses invite us to be "good" within the framework of an inhuman world, Lao Tzu rejects this world and its premises. He invites us to transcend every false premise of our culture, and to be reborn in the form of our essential humanity, which needs no tests of performance, wealth, achievement or goodness to validate itself. From Lao Tzu's point of view, not even a guidebook is required. The *Tao Te Ching* is more likely to have been the product of many generations of Lao Tzu's disciples.

Lao Tzu is keenly aware that the rules we live by interfere with our essential beingness. He invites us to emancipate ourselves from these rules and suggests that this very act is a key which unlocks the door to our self-realization.

He holds that we are deserving regardless of our achievements or contributions. We deserve to fulfill our material and our spiritual needs simply because we are human beings, and certainly not because we fulfill the conditionalities that our manipulative institutions demand. Twenty-seven centuries later, we are at last pregnant with a post-civilized world modeled after Lao Tzu's main premises. Indeed, he was certainly an extraordinarily prophetic man.

THE GREAT INTEGRITY IS LOVE

The Great Integrity is love. It is the love that uniquely expresses our deepest unarmored bonds with each other. On the highest level we become love. Our language, like all other aspects of our culture, tends to obfuscate our loss of wholeness and humanity. Since the experience of love requires this very wholeness and humanity that we have for the most part lost, our use of the term most often refers to the perversions of love that are compensatory for this loss. We might differentiate five types of love. The first three are pathological contradictions of the Great Integrity, and the last two are healthy expressions of it.

The first type is *possessive love* – that is, loving an object because we are capable of possessing it, or at least believing that we possess it. Even one's mate might be loved as an object. This is the most alienated form of love and is widely practiced, since the civilizations of the past 5,000 years have been focused on possessing. All objects are viewed for their value to exchange and accumulate. Success is defined as the power to accrue and maintain the largest number of desirable objects. People too are objectified, primarily as the means to create the objects to be acquired, so control over those who produce those objects becomes a basic test of success. The objectification of nature and of human labor, when extended to personal relations, takes many forms – for example, male chauvinism, which is a typical expression of love as possession. Clearly, objective love is not only toxic to our humanity, but inverts and perverts the very act of loving itself, turning it from a selfless and spontaneous experience of human fulfillment to a selfish and manipulative act.

The second type of love is sometimes referred to as *codependent love*. It is rooted in the experience of powerlessness and expresses itself as an addiction to control or being controlled. A relationship of codependent love is a struggle for competing dependencies and results in the mutual exploitation of immaturities. Codependency prevents self-growth and independence, as well as genuine fulfillments. It is also a contradiction of the Great Integrity but on a lesser level than the first, possessive type of love.

The third type of love might be called *romantic love*. It is generally an unconscious escapist attempt to compensate for the absence of self-appreciation. It is therefore generally a search for that "perfect" mate who is imagined as having the qualities that the romantic lover lacks. Although less pathological than possessive or codependent love, romantic love also contradicts the Great Integrity by its compensatory functions that drive a wedge between the essential self and the imagined deficient self, as well as between the essential other and the imagined "perfect" mate.

The fourth type of love is *subjective love*. It is the expression of a state of lovingness. There are no ulterior motives, no objects of material value to be acquired. The person who experiences subjective love is relatively without armor. Love is freely given and received. In such love, we are not fixated on a single possessive or codependent or romantic object of our love, but we love, and are loved by many people. Moreover, in subjective love, not only human beings, but animals, birds, plants, rocks, art, the entire gamut of nature and of the environment – the entire universe – tend to be experienced in a loving way. In this fourth form of love, many layers of armoring are shed, and we live more in harmony with each other, with nature and with our own human natures. It is the healthiest and most fulfilling level of love that our present epoch of transition offers as a potential expression of the Great Integrity.

In the fifth type, we will experience love beyond its objective and subjective forms. We will *become love*. It is the experience of our total humanity, stripped of every shred of alienation, stripped of every premise of aggressive civilization. It is complete self- and social actualization. Indeed, it is the ideal state of being that Lao Tzu defines as the Great Integrity, and is realizable only in the Third Epoch.

As long as we live within acquisitive societies, we will be deprived of the fifth type of love, which is to say that all of us today are incapable of fully experiencing the Great Integrity. Within civilization, the Great Integrity can only be dreamed, sensed and vicariously or tentatively experienced. It cannot define the everyday experiential core of our being until we live an alternative life style that has completely healed the divisions between privileged and underprivileged, left and right brain, between us and them, and between the ego us and the id us. The Great Integrity requires the transcendence of all the fragmentations that have defined our personal and social lives during the past few millennia. Lao Tzu's Great Integrity is nothing less than the total liberation of each and all of us to experience this universe on its own terms, transcending all objectivities and subjectivities while never having to sacrifice our humanity – that is, our ability to function with a higher consciousness than the rest of nature.

Such a state is difficult for us to imagine since it lies so beyond the capabilities of our everyday experience which is still locked in the chains of civilization. At this point in time, Lao Tzu's *Guide to the Theory and Practice of the Great Integrity* allows us a closer look at our future, a clearer glimpse of its shapes and feelings, and an insight into our own uncorrupted Essence that is reborn on a higher level each moment that we take another step toward our own emancipation.

* * * * *

HOW I WROTE THIS BOOK

My Chinese is much too rudimentary to have directly translated the *Tao Te Ching* from Chinese to English. I mainly relied upon two different manuscripts that provided translations of the multiple English equivalents of each Chinese character of the 81 sections. One manuscript was written for me by Professor Yan Cheng[21] who assisted me for 12 years, researching publications written only in Chinese, providing English–Chinese and Chinese–English translations, and computerizing my manuscripts in preparation for publication.

The other translation was written by Chi Choo-Li in collaboration with my friend, Mark Johnson,[22] one of the leading authorities in the U.S. on Qi Gong, Feng Shui and ancient Chinese philosophy. Also useful was the Chinese–English character-by-character translation by Gregory C. Richter, although this book provides only one English meaning for each Chinese character.[23] Lastly, I was fortunate to have discovered Jonathan Star's scholarly work before completing my manuscript. Star lists the multiple possible meanings of each character.[24] I was also grateful for the 28 English translations of the *Tao Te Ching* that are part of my own personal library.[25]

My criteria in the translations were:

(1) To offer the most poetic translations in English that I could. Although the original Chinese is written more as prose than poetry, I felt that the central ideas, being more paradoxical than logical, demanded a language that transcended language, and that task fundamentally requires poetry.

(2) To create a consistency and integrity for each of the 81 verses. Although the original manuscript consisted of a single 5,000-character document, almost all translators have accepted the later 81 section divisions. I felt that this division is useful and practical, offering the reader a potential special meditative focus for each section. I have supported this 81-part division in three main ways: a) By shaping a thematic constancy within each verse; b) By giving a title to each verse that identifies its particular focus; and c) By allowing the last stanza to serve as a summary of the main implications of the verse.

(3) To make a language bridge between Lao Tzu's intent and its specific meanings for us today.

All of the above is to say that, because in the Great Integrity we are all inseparable, in the following pages I invite you as a friend to join me in an amazing adventure that allows us to tune into Lao Tzu's wisdom of two and a half millennia ago as a song that he is singing to each and all of us, as though he were living in our own hearts, dreams and alternatives.

Ralph Alan Dale

TAO
TE
CHING
THE VERSES

1

Transcending

The Tao that can be told
is not the universal Tao.
The name that can be named
is not the universal name.

In the infancy of the universe,
there were no names.
Naming fragments the mysteries of life
into ten thousand things and their manifestations.

Yet mysteries and manifestations
spring from the same source:
The Great Integrity
which is the mystery within manifestation,
the manifestation within mystery,
the naming of the unnamed,
and the un-naming of the named.

When these interpenetrations
are in full attendance,
we will pass the gates of naming notions
in our journey toward transcendence.

老子

道可道非常道名可名非常名無名天地之始
有名萬物之母常無欲以觀其妙常有欲以觀
其徼此而者同出而異名同謂之玄玄之又玄眾
妙之門

2
Relativity

We know beauty because there is ugly.
We know good because there is evil.
Being and not being,
having and not having,
create each other.

Difficult and easy,
long and short,
high and low,
define each other,
just as before and after follow each other.

The dialectic of sound gives voice to music,
always transforming "is" from "was"
as the ancestors of "to be".

The wise
teach without telling,
allow without commanding,
have without possessing,
care without claiming.

In this way we harvest eternal importance
because we never announce it.

天下皆知美之為美斯惡已皆知善之為善斯不
善已故有無之相生難易之相成長短之相形高
下之相傾音聲之相和前後之相隨是以聖人處
無為之事行不言之教萬物作而不辭生而不
有為而不恃功成不居夫唯不居是以不去

Tempering

Overpraising the gifted leads to contentiousness.
Overvaluing the precious invites stealing.
Craving the desirable loses contentment.

The natural person
desires without craving
and acts without excess.

By not doing,
everything is done.

者不敢為也為無為則無不治矣

其腹弱其志強其骨常使民無知無欲使夫知

盜不見可欲使心不亂是以聖人之治也虛其心實

不尚賢使民不爭不貴難得之偵使民不為

4
The Great Integrity

The Great Integrity is an endless abyss,
Yet it is the inexhaustibly fertile
source of the universe.

It blunts all sharpness,
unties the entangled,
and merges with the dust!

Hidden but ever present –
this parent of the gods –
Whose child may it be?

道沖而用之或不盈淵乎似萬物之宗挫其銳
解其紛和其光同其塵湛兮似若存吾不知
其誰之子象帝之先

5

Yin and Yang

Yin and yang aren't sentimental.
They exist without moralizing.
They act regardless of our wishes
within the ebb and flow
of every pregnant moment.

The space between yin and yang
is like a bellows –
empty, yet infinitely full.
The more it yields,
the more it fills.

Countless words
count less
than the silent balance
between yin and yang.

天地不仁以萬物為芻狗聖人不仁以百姓為芻
狗天地之間其猶橐籥乎虛而不屈動而愈
出多言數窮不如守中

Life's Spirit

The spirit of life
never dies.

It is the infinite gateway
to mysteries within mysteries.

It is the seed of yin,
the spark of yang.

Always elusive,
endlessly available.

谷神不死是謂玄牝玄牝之門是謂天地根綿綿若存用之不勤

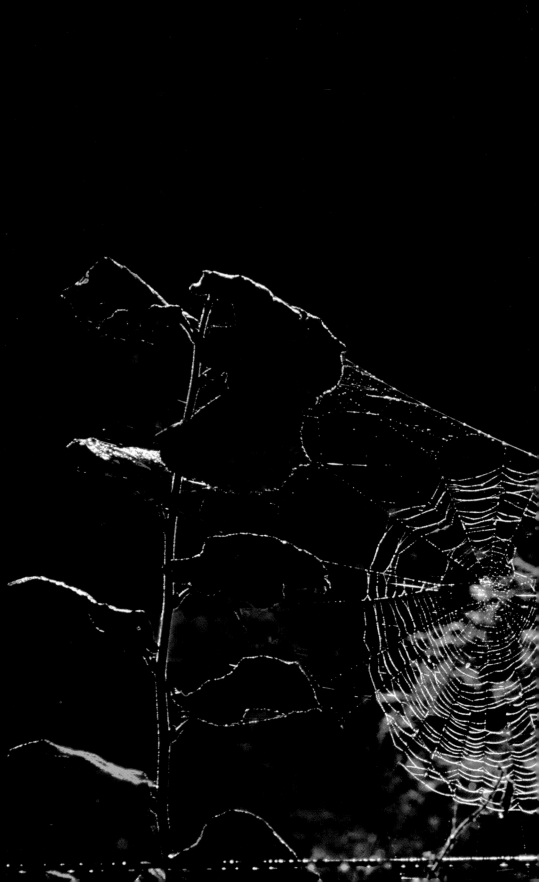

7
Modesty

The Great Integrity, having had no birth,
expresses its immortality
without pronouncements.

The wise are heard
through their silence,
always self-full through selflessness.

天長地久天地所以能長且久者以其不自生故
能長生是以聖人後其身而身先外其身而身
存非以其無私耶故能成其私

8
The Highest Good

The highest good is like water,
nourishing life effortlessly,
flowing without prejudice
to the lowliest places.

It springs from all
who nourish their community
with a benevolent heart as deep as an abyss,
who are incapable of lies and injustices,
who are rooted in the earth,
and whose natural rhythms of action
play midwife to the highest good
of each pregnant moment.

政善治事善能動善時夫惟不爭故無尤矣

惡故幾於道居善地心善淵與善人言善信

上善若水水善利萬物而不爭處眾人之所

9
Overfulfillment

Keep filling your bowl,
and it will spill over.

Keep sharpening your knife,
and it will blunt.

Keep hoarding gold in your house,
and you will be robbed.

Keep seeking approval,
and you will be chained.

The Great Integrity leads to actualization,
never overfulfillment.

持而盈之不如其已揣而銳不可長保金玉滿堂莫之能守富貴而驕自遺其咎功成名遂身退天之道

10
Limitations

When embracing the unity
of mind, body, emotions and spiritual being,
can we transcend our fragmentations
without leaving a trace?

When Qi Gong sculpts sinew suppleness,
can our flesh become soft as a newborn babe?

Can we cleanse the inner vision,
leaving mind in spiritual purity?

Can our affairs of the heart,
and our affairs of state,
be so unconditional
that we grant unqualified permissibility?

Can the gate to Yin be opened
without inviting Yang?

Can our reasoning mind be purged of coercion,
allowing our heart its unfettered joy?

Can we act like every other species,
seeking no reward,
taking no pride,
guiding without enslaving?

Such is our vision of the Great Integrity
on whose path we have at last planted both feet,
ready to move, step by step,
until we arrive at the great unfettered gate.

載營魄抱一能無離乎專氣致柔能如嬰兒
乎滌除玄覽能無疵乎愛民治國能無為乎
天門開闔能無雌乎明白四達能無知乎生之
畜之生而不有為而不恃長而不宰是謂玄德

11

The Importance of
What Is Not

We join thirty spokes
to the hub of a wheel,
yet it's the center hole
that drives the chariot.

We shape clay
to birth a vessel,
yet it's the hollow within
that makes it useful.

We chisel doors and windows
to construct a room,
yet it's the inner space
that makes it livable.

Thus do we
create what is
to use what is not.

三十輻共一轂當其無有車之用埏埴以為器當其無有器之用鑿戶牖以為室當其無有室之用故有之以為利無之以為用

12
Choices

Colors can make us blind!
Music can make us deaf!
Flavors can destroy our taste!
Possessions can dose our options!
Racing can drive us mad
and its rewards obstruct our peace!

Thus, the wise
fill the inner gut
rather than the eyes,
always sacrificing the superficial
for the essential.

五色令人目盲五音令人耳聾五味令人口爽
馳騁田獵令人心發狂難得之貨令人行妨是
以聖人為腹不為目故去彼取此

13

Identity

Accolades can usher in
great trouble for your body.
Censure can herald misery.

Why can favor and disfavor
both be harmful?

Because both accolades and censure,
when filtered through self as ego,
always place us in jeopardy.

But when the universe becomes your self,
when you love the world as yourself,
all reality becomes your haven,
reinventing you as your own heaven.

Only then, will you transcend tense
to fully be here now.
Only then, no harm
will the universe proffer
nor you to her,
for you will be
not you but she
and both – the universal Great Integrity.

寵辱若驚貴大患若身何謂寵辱寵為下得
之若驚失之若驚是謂寵辱若驚何謂貴大
患若身吾所以有大患者為吾有身及吾無身
吾有何患故貴以身為天下若可寄天下愛以
身為天下若可託天下

14

Beyond Reason

That which we look at
but cannot see is the invisible.

That which we listen to
but cannot hear is the inaudible.

That which we reach for
but cannot grasp is the intangible.

Beyond reason, these three merge,
contradicting experience.

Their rising side isn't bright.
Their setting side isn't dark.

Sense-less, unnamable, they return
to the realms of nothingness.

Form without form,
image without image,
indefinable, ineluctable, elusive.

Confronting them, you see no beginning.
Following them, you see no end.

Yet, riding the plowless plow
can seed the timeless Tao,
harvesting the secret
transcendence of the Now.

古始是謂道紀
首隨之不見其後執古之道以御今之有能知
無狀之狀無物之象是謂忽恍迎之不見其
瞰其不不昧繩繩不可名復歸於無物是謂
名曰微此三者不可致詰故混而為一其上不
視之不見名曰夷聽之不聞名曰希搏之不得

15

Linking with Ancient Times

In ancient times
the people knew the Great Integrity
with subtlety and profundity.

Because they are so unfathomable to us,
we can describe the ancients
only with great effort.

They were –
cautious as those crossing an icy stream,
wary as those surrounded by dangers,
dignified as guests,
yielding as melting ice,
innocent as virgin wood,
open and broad as valleys,
merging freely as muddy water.

But today, who can remain patient
while the mud so gradually clears?
Who can remain still
while the moment for action
so slowly emerges?

Who?
We observers of the Great Integrity,
who in our times,
like those ancients,
never seeking fulfillment,
are never unfulfilled.

古之善為士者微妙玄通深不可識夫惟不可識故強為之容豫芳若冬涉川猶芳若畏四邻微芳其若容渙兮若冰將釋敦芳其若樸曠兮其若谷沖芳其若濁孰能濁以靜之徐清孰能安以動之徐生保此道者不欲盈夫惟不盈故能弊不新成

30

16
Tranquility

Allow the heart to empty itself of all turmoil!
Retrieve the utter tranquility of mind
from which you issued.

Although all forms are dynamic,
and we all grow and transform,
each of us is compelled to return to our root.
Our root is quietude.

To fully return to our root is to be enlightened.
Never to experience tranquility is to act blindly,
a sure path to disaster.

To know tranquility is to embrace all.
To embrace all is to be just.
Justice is the foundation for wholeness.
Wholeness is the Great Integrity.
The Great Integrity is the infinite fulfilling itself.

致虛極守靜篤萬物並作吾以觀其復夫物
芸芸各歸其根歸根曰靜靜曰復命復命曰
常知常曰明不知常妄作凶知常容容乃公公
乃王王乃天天乃道道乃久沒身不殆

17
Leaders

There are four types of leaders:
The best leader is indistinguishable
from the will of those who selected her.
The next best leader enjoys the love
and praise of the people.
The poor leader rules through coercion and fear.
And the worst leader is a tyrant despised
by the multitudes who are the victims of his power.

What a world of difference among these leaders!
In the last two types, what is done
is without sincerity or trust – only coercion.
In the second type, there is a harmony
between the leader and the people.
In the first type, whatever is done happens
so naturally that no one presumes to take the credit!

太上下知有之其次親之譽之其次畏之侮之故
信不足焉有不信猶兮其貴言功成事遂百
姓皆謂我自然

18

The Paradoxes of Abandoning the Great Integrity

When the Great Integrity was abandoned,
humanity and justice appeared.

When knowledge and teachers appeared,
hypocrisy was their inevitable accompaniment.

When family relationships lost their harmony,
filial piety and parental affection were suddenly birthed.

When a nation succumbs to chaos and corruption,
patriotic politicians are always at hand announcing themselves.

孝
慈
國
家
昏
亂
有
忠
臣

大
道
廢
有
仁
義
智
惠
出
有
大
偽
六
親
不
和
有

19

The Paradoxes of Returning to the Great Integrity

Banish the intellectual!
Discard knowledge!
We will all benefit a hundredfold!

Eliminate all institutions of charity and justice!
We can then return
to our natural love for each other.

Let everyone be released
from our addictions to shrewdness and profit!
Then, thievery will disappear!

These three negate the Great Integrity.
But to negate these negations is insufficient.
Three affirmations are also necessary.

The first is to embrace simplicity and integrity.
The second is to consume only the needs of our body and soul.
The third is to allow our love and concern for others to define our essentiality.

絕聖棄智民利百倍絕仁棄義民復孝慈
絕巧棄利盜賊無有此三者以為文不足故
令有所屬見素抱樸少私寡欲

20

The Sadness of Superficialities
and of the Unfulfilled Great Integrity

It is sometimes deeply depressing to be a rebel,
knowing that we can never share most people's way of life, nor can they share ours.

Schooling stuffs the brains of our children with trivia.
The more the trivia, the more their anxieties.
They indoctrinate the children to believe that the consequences are grave
when they fail to distinguish "good" from "evil", and agreement from disagreement.
What gross nonsense!

To escape the rubbish of all this so-called knowledge,
in the winter people run to the great feasts of lamb, pork and ox,
and they climb high in the mountains to view the first signs of spring.

We are so different! Having no desire for the trivialities,
nor for their compensations, we are like infants not yet knowing how to laugh!
Ever wandering, and having no home to which we may return.

While most people are obsessed with superficialities, we feel empty.
While most people feel they know so much, we feel simple-minded.
While most people believe they live happily in the best of all possible worlds,
we are despaired to witness this world!
It is so painful to know that we will always be outsiders,
endlessly moving like the ocean, aimlessly blowing like the wind.

While we fear what others fear, we don't treasure what others treasure.
Our treasure is the Great Integrity.
However, until it is shared, it will not be the Universal Integrity,
for we are part of them, and they are part of us.

絕學無憂唯之與阿相去幾何善之與惡相
去何若人之所畏不可不畏荒兮其未央哉眾
人熙熙如享太牢如登春臺我獨泊兮其未兆
若嬰兒之未孩乘乘兮若無所歸眾人皆有
餘我獨若遺我愚人之心也哉沌沌兮俗人昭
昭我獨若昏俗人察察我獨悶悶澹兮其
若海飂兮似無所止眾人皆有以我獨頑似鄙
我獨異於人而貴求食於母

21

The Great Integrity Is a Paradox

The Great Integrity is a paradox.
It is inherent in the universe,
yet its form is so elusive.
It is the Vital Essence of every entity,
yet nothing announces its essential character.

The Great Integrity was apparent
before time, space and matter appeared
    to separate.
How can we re-mind and re-infuse ourselves
with this very touchstone of all essentialities
    and connections?

By re-fusing time, space and matter
with the spiritualization of our materiality,
and with the materialization of our spirituality.

Then, when our dualities and numeralities
become blurred and forgotten,
the Great Integrity will re-emerge in forms
of such incredible depths and dimensions
    of enlightenment,
precisely because our temporary fragmentary
    consciousness
created a multi-millennial amnesia.

孔德之容惟道是從道之為物惟恍惟惚
惚兮恍其中有象恍兮惚其中有物窈兮
冥兮其中有精其精甚真其中有信自古
及今其名不去以閱眾甫吾何以知眾甫之
然哉以此

22

Celebrate Paradox!

No-thing remains itself.
Each prepares the path to its opposite.

To be ready for wholeness, first be fragmented.
To be ready for rightness, first be wronged.
To be ready for fullness, first be empty.
To be ready for renewal, first be worn out.
To be ready for success, first fail.
To be ready for doubt, first be certain.

Because the wise observe the world
through the Great Integrity,
they know they are not knowledgeable.
Because they do not perceive
only through their perceptions,
they do not judge this right and that wrong.
Because they do not delight in boasting,
they are appreciated.
Because they do not announce their superiority,
they are acclaimed.
Because they never compete,
no one can compete with them.

Verily, fragmentation prepares the path to wholeness,
the mother of all origins and realizations.

者 不 自 則 曲
豈 爭 是 惑 則
虛 故 故 是 全
言 天 彰 以 枉
哉 下 不 聖 則
故 莫 自 人 直
誠 能 伐 抱 窪
全 與 故 一 則
而 之 有 為 盈
歸 爭 功 天 弊
之 古 不 下 則
　 之 自 式 新
　 所 矜 不 少
　 謂 故 自 則
　 曲 長 見 得
　 則 夫 故 多
　 全 惟 明 則
　 　 不 不 惑

44

希言自然飄風不終朝驟雨不終日孰為此
者天地天地尚不能久而況於人乎故從事
於道者道者同於道德者同於德失者同
於失同於道者道亦得之同於德者德亦得
之同於失者失亦得之信不足焉有不信焉
政者不立跨者不行自見者不明自是者不
彰自伐者無功自矜者不長其於道也曰餘
食贅行物或惡之故有道者不處也

23
Sincerity

Speak few words, but say them with quietude and sincerity,
and they will be long-lasting,
for a raging wind cannot blow all morning,
nor a sudden rainstorm last throughout the day.

Why is this so?
Because it is the nature of the sky and the earth to be frugal.
Even human beings cannot alter this nature
without suffering the consequences.

When we sincerely follow the ethical path,
we become one with it.
When we become one with the ethical path, it embraces us.

When we completely lose our way, we become one with loss.
When we become one with loss, loss embraces us.

When we sincerely follow the Great Integrity,
we become one with it.
When we are one with the Great Integrity, it embraces us.

But when nothing is done sincerely,
no-thing and no one embraces us.

24

Avoiding Voids

Standing on tiptoe will only make you tipsy,
Walking with long strides will not allow a long walk.
Shining the light on yourself will never enlighten you.
Being self-righteous precludes you from being right.
Boasting about yourself will never boost your eminence.
Parading yourself parodies leadership.

Tao consciousness avoids
the cultivation of all these ego-bloated voids.

食贅行物或惡之故有道者不處也
彰自伐者無功自矜者不長其於道也曰餘
政者不立跨者不行自見者不明自是者不

25

Naming the Nameless

What preceded life? The earth.
What preceded the earth? The universe.
What preceded the universe?
The soundless and shapeless, origin of origins,
ever transforming and having no beginning
    nor end.

This Mother of the universe is boundless,
    and nameless.
But if we wanted to share with you anything
about this remarkable non-executing executor,
we must invent a name for it.

We will call it the Tao because Tao means great.
Incredibly great because it occupies infinite space,
being fully present in the whole universe, and in
    every infinitesimal particle.

Because this Great Integrity created the universe,
and the universe created the earth,
and the earth created us, we are all incredibly great.

Life derives from the nature of the earth.
The earth derives from the nature of the universe.
The universe derives from the nature of the Great Integrity.
And the Great Integrity is the omnipresent, omnigenous omniform,
the universal material and spiritual substance,
and the holoversal interlinkage and coition of existence.

有物混成先天地生寂兮寥兮獨立而不改

周行而不殆可以為天下母吾不知其名字之

曰道強為之名曰大大曰逝逝曰遠遠曰返故

道大天大地大王亦大域中有四大而王居

其一焉人法地地法天天法道道法自然

50

26

Seductions

Inner strength is the master
of all frivolities.
Tranquility is the master
of all agitated emotions.

Those who succumb to frivolities
have lost their inner strength.
Those who succumb to agitated emotions
have lost their tranquility.

The wise cultivate
inner strength and tranquility.
That is why they are not seduced
by addictive temptations.

而以身輕天下輕則失臣躁則失君
輜重雖有榮觀燕處超然奈何萬乘之主
重為輕根靜為躁君是以君子終日行不離

27

Wisdom is Effortless Mutuality

善行無轍迹善言無瑕讁善計不用籌策
善開無關楗而不可開善結無繩約而不可
解是以聖人常善救人故無棄人常善救物
故無棄物是謂襲明故善人不善人之師不
善人善人之資不貴其師不愛其資雖智大
迷是謂要妙

The expert traveler leaves no footprints.
The expert speaker makes no mispronunciations.
The expert in calculation needs no calculator.

The expert in closing things needs no lock,
yet no one can open what has been closed.
The expert in binding uses no knots,
yet no one can pull apart what has
    been bound.

The expert in caring for things never
    wastes anything.
The expert at helping people never
    abandons anyone.

These are the paths to enlightenment.
Those who arrive at their destination
teach those who are still on the path,
while those still on the path
are sources of wisdom for the teachers.

28

The Fusion of Opposites

To know the masculine and be true to the feminine
is to be the waterway of the world.

To be the waterway of the world is to flow with the Great Integrity,
always swirling back to the innocence of childhood.

To know yang and to be true to yin is
to echo the universe.

To echo the universe is to merge with the Great Integrity,
ever returning to the infinite.

To know praise and be true to the lowly
is to be a model for the planet.

To be a model for the planet is to express the Great Integrity
as the Primal Simplicity – like an uncarved block.

When the uncarved block goes to the craftsman,
it is transformed into something useful.

The wise craftsman cuts as little as necessary
because he follows the Great Integrity.

知其雄守其雌為天下谿為天下谿常德不
離復歸於嬰兒知其白守其黑為天下式為天
下式常德不忒復歸於無極知其榮守其辱
為天下谷為天下谷常德乃足復歸於樸散
則為器聖人用之則為官長故大制不割

29
We Are the World

Those who have most power and wealth
treat the planet as a thing to be possessed,
to be used and abused according to their own dictates.
But the planet is a living organism,
a Great Spiritual Integrity.

To violate this Integrity
is certain to cull forth disaster
since each and every one of us
is an inherent part
of this very organism.

All attempts to control the world
can only lead to its decimation
and to our own demise
since we are an inseparable part
of what we are senselessly trying to coerce.

Any attempt to possess the world
can only lead to its loss
and to our own dissolution
since we are an intrinsic part
of what we are foolishly trying to possess.

The world's pulse is our pulse.
The world's rhythms are our rhythms.
To treat our planet with care, moderation and love
is to be in synchrony with ourselves
and to live in the Great Integrity.

将欲取天下而為之者吾見其不得已天下神
器不可為也為者敗之執者失之故物或行
或随或煦或吹或强或羸或載或隳是以聖
人去甚去奢去泰

30
Defense and Aggression

Those on the path of the Great Integrity
never use military force to conquer others.
Every aggressive act harvests its own counter-terrorism.

Wherever the military marches,
the killing fields lay waste to the land,
yielding years of famine and misery.

When attacked, those on the path of the
    Great Integrity
defend themselves benevolently,
never revenging.

Achieve success without arrogance,
without seeking glory,
and without violating others.

Aggression leaches our strength and humanity,
subverting the Great Integrity,
and inviting disaster.

以道佐人主者不以兵強天下其事好還師之
所處荊棘生焉大軍之後必有凶年故善
者果而已不敢以取強焉果而勿矜果而勿
伐果而勿驕果而不得已果而勿強物壯則
老是謂不道不道早已

31

War

The finest weapons are the worst evils.
They are universally loathed.
Therefore, help guide your nation to the non-aggressive path.

The wise hold steady on the passive yin path.
Those who are aggressive prefer the active yang.

Weapons are instruments of coercion and devils of death.
Resort to them only in dire necessity.
Peace is our natural state of being.

If weapons must be wielded to defend ourselves,
and we are victorious, never rejoice.
Can there be joy over the slaughter of others?

On joyous occasions,
we attune with the yang side.
On sad occasions, with the yin.

During battle, the soldiers are on the left yang side,
engaging in the combat.
The commanders are on the right yin side,
observing the action.

After the battle, the soldiers who have slain others,
move to the yin side and mourn,
while the commanders, now on the yang side,
are celebrating victory even though it is a funeral.

夫佳兵者不祥之器物或惡之故有道者不
處君子居則貴左用兵則貴右兵者不祥之
器非君子之器不得已而用之恬淡為上勝
而不美而美之者是樂殺人夫樂殺人者不可
得志於天下矣吉事尚左凶事尚右是以偏將
軍處左上將軍處右言居上勢則以喪禮
處之殺人眾多則以悲哀泣之戰勝則以喪
禮處之道常無名樸雖小天下莫能臣侯王

32

Is It Not Time to Unify the Fragments?

Although the Great Integrity is infinite,
and therefore undefined,
It is silent in its Primal Simplicity.

Nothing is its superior.
When humanity embraces the Great Integrity,
all life on earth will be grateful.

All yin and yang will be harmonized
in the sweet daily dew, and peace will reign
on the planet without anyone commanding it.

When the Primal Simplicity atomized
into the 10,000 fragments, with their 10,000 names,
our planet became endangered.

Now – are there not enough fragments?
Is it not time to stop and return to the universal sea
from which all streams emerged?

To return to the Great Integrity
is to obliterate
the list of the 10,000 endangered species.

江海也
莫之令而自均始制有名名亦既有夫亦將知
以知止所以不殆臂道之在天下猶川谷之於
若能守萬物將自賓天地相合以降甘露人

33
Who Are You?

If you understand others, you are astute.
If you understand yourself, you are insightful.

If you master others, you are uncommonly forceful.
If you master yourself, you have uncommon inner strength.

If you know when you have enough, you are wealthy.
If you carry your intentions to completion, you are resolute.

If you find your roots and nourish them, you will know longevity.
If you live a long creative life, you will leave an eternal legacy.

壽知人者智自知者明勝人者有力自勝者強知
之者富強行者有志不失其所久死而不亡者

34

Humility and Greatness

The Great Integrity is unboundable like a flood.
It cannot be manipulated this or that way.
It is the very wellspring of life,
always outpouring, never commanding.

Although the source for every need,
it is never demanding.
It does work silently
and unpretentiously.

All return to the Great Integrity
as our liberating universal home.
By never seeking greatness,
greatness permeates in deed.

大道汎兮其可左右萬物恃之以生而不辭功
成不居衣被萬物而不為主故常無欲可名
於小矣萬物歸焉而不知主可名於大矣是
以聖人能成其大也以其不自大故能成其大

35

The Consummate Food
and the Ultimate Music

When you merge with the universe,
the whole world is attracted to you,
discovering through you
its own security, peace and good health.

Passing guests may stop by – at first attracted
to your savory food and inspirational music.
But they might leave more deeply enriched
than they could have anticipated –

Because the silent song of Tao
is the ultimate music,
and the infinite delicacy of Tao
is the consummate nourishment.

執大象天下往往而不害安平泰樂與餌過
容止道之出口淡乎其無味視之不足見聽之
不足聞用之不可既

36

Too Much Invites Disaster

What is overexpanded becomes diminished.
What is too strong becomes weakened.
What is too high is cut down.
What is overpossessed becomes impoverished.

It is in the nature of process that in the final stages,
those who are overextended,
overarmed and overprivileged,
shall be overcome.

Disaster stalks the fish
which swims up from its deep water home,
and the army which threatens to conquer
those beyond its own borders.

將欲歙之必固張之將欲
弱之必固強之將欲廢之必固興之將欲奪之必固與之是謂微明
柔弱勝剛強魚不可脫於淵國之利器不
可以示人道常無為而無不為侯王若能守萬

37

The Primal Simplicity

The Great Integrity imposes no action,
yet it leaves nothing undone.
Were governments to embrace it,
everything would develop naturally.

If thereafter an old ego should reincarnate,
the already permeated Primal Simplicity
would neutralize it in its pervasive silence.

Returning to silence is returning to peace.
Returning to peace, the world reharmonizes itself.

物將自化；而欲作吾將鎮之以無名之樸無
名之樸亦將不欲不欲以靜天下將自正

Distinguishing the Highest
from the Lowest Morality

You can readily recognize the highest virtuousness
because it never places itself on display.
You can readily recognize the lowest virtuousness
because it is always announcing itself.

The highest virtue quietly serves universal needs.
The lowest virtue actively strives for personal success.
The highest morality serves common needs.
The lowest morality is self-serving.

True benevolence
acts without intention.
But when rituals go unheeded,
they are enforced with rolled-up sleeves.

Failing the Great Integrity, we resort to virtuousness.
Failing virtuousness, we resort to moralizing.
Failing moralizing, we resort to dogma,
the most superficial form of faith and loyalty,
and the nourishment for confusion.

Natural persons are attracted
to substance rather than form,
to the nutritious fruit rather than the enticing flower,
to that which dwells deeply within,
rather than to that which clings superficially to the surface.

上德不德，是以有德；下德不失德，是以無德。上德無為而無以為；下德為之而有以為。上仁為之而無以為；上義為之而有以為。上禮為之而莫之應，則攘臂而仍之。故失道而後德，失德而後仁，失仁而後義，失義而後禮。夫禮者，忠信之薄，而亂之首也。前識者，道之華，而愚之始也。是以大丈夫處其厚，不居其薄；居其實，不居其華。故去彼取此。

77

昔之得一者天得一以清地得一以寧神得一
以靈谷得一以盈萬物得一以生侯王得一以
為天下貞其致之一也天無以清將恐裂地無
以寧將恐發神無以靈將恐歇谷無以盈將
恐竭萬物無以生將恐滅侯王無以為貞而貴
高將恐蹶故貴以賤為本高以下為基是以侯
王自稱孤寡不穀此其以賤為本耶非乎
故致數譽無譽不欲琭琭如玉珞珞如石

39
Then and Now

In ancient times, all entities had their own integrity and function.
The sky was clear and endless.
The earth was calm and firm.
The gods were charged with spiritual powers.
The wells were clean and full.
The 10,000 creatures were healthy and fecund.
Leaders were elected to plan the work and defense of the community.
How wondrously concordant!

If the sky were not endless, it could have fallen.
If the earth were not firm, it could have burst.
If the gods did not exercise their spiritual powers,
they would have been abandoned.
If the wells were not full, they could have dried up.
If the 10,000 creatures were not productive,
they could have become extinct.
If the leaders did not plan the work and defense of the community,
they would have been replaced.
In this way, each entity had its own essentiality,
each part complementing every other.

Nowadays, when the privileged among us identify themselves
with the orphan, the widower and the hungry one,
it may be an opportunistic appeal for the support of the lowly,
or a realization that loudly trumpeting self-glory negates itself,
or a premonition that shining like jade, and resounding like stone chimes
attracts the desperate adventurers among those deprived of hope,
inviting disaster among those who create these deprivations.

40

All Is Paradox

反者道之動弱者道之用天下之物生於有

有生於無

The movement of the Great Integrity is infinite,
yet its character is passive.
Being defines every form of life,
yet all originate in, and return to, non-being.

上士聞道勤而行之中士聞道若存若亡下
士聞道大笑之不笑不足以為道故建言
有之明道若昧夷道若纇進道若退上德
若谷大白若辱廣德若不足建德若偷質
真若渝大方無隅大器晚成大音希聲大
象無形道隱無名夫惟道善貸且成

41

Observing and Nourishing Paradox

When most people hear about the Great Integrity,
they waiver between belief and disbelief.
When wise people hear about the Great Integrity,
they diligently follow its path.
When ignorant people hear about it,
they laugh out loud!
By this very laughter, we know its authenticity.

It is said that –
enlightenment appears dark,
the progressive way appears retrograde,
the smooth way appears jagged,
the highest peak of revelation appears empty like a valley,
the cleanest appears to be soiled,
the greatest abundance appears insufficient,
the most enduring inner strength appears like weakness,
creativity appears imitative.

Great talents mature slowly.
Great sounds are silent.
Great forms look shapeless.
Transcendent squareness has no corners.

The Great Integrity hides behind all forms,
stubbornly nourishing the paradoxes that can enlighten us.

42
The Principles of Transformation

The Great Integrity expresses one.
One manifests as two.
Two is transformed into three.
And three generates all the myriad entities of the universe.

Every entity always returns to yin after engaging yang.
The fusion of these two opposites
births the Vital Energy that sustains the harmony of life.

But for most people, this harmony is decimated
by inheriting a condition
of relative misery, scarcity and victimization.

Politicians cleverly pretend that they too originate
from the toxic soil of this misery,
even while designing the very laws
that legitimate victimization.

But watch out – those who hoard oversufficiency
will be diminished!
And those who are diminished
will become bountiful!

These commonly known truths
that common people teach each other,
are also my truths.

As you sow, so shall you reap.
Such is the heart of my teaching
in a world forced to live heartlessly.

道生一一生二二生三三生萬物萬物負陰而抱
陽沖氣以為和人之所惡唯孤寡不穀而王公
以為稱故物或損之而益或益之而損人之所
教亦我義教之強梁者不得其死吾將以為
教父。

43

The Value of Minimums

That which is most tender
can overcome that which is most rigid.
That which has least substance
can penetrate that which has least space.

Acting without deliberate action,
and teaching without uttering a word,
are rarely practiced.
So few find their way to the Great Integrity!

天下之至柔馳騁天下之至堅無有入於無間

吾是以知無為之有益不言之教無為之益天

下希及之

44
Choices

Which do you value more –
your wealth or your wellness?
Which is more harmful –
to lead or to lose?

The greater is your attachment,
the more bereft is your release.
The more you hoard,
the less is left to enjoy.

Those on the path
to the Great Integrity
flow without forcing,
leaving no space for disasters.

名與身孰親身與貨孰多得與亡孰病是故
甚愛必大費多藏必厚亡知足不辱知止不
殆可以長久

45
Illusion and Reality

Completeness can seem incomplete,
yet the completeness that we achieve can be remarkable.
Fullness can seem empty,
yet the fullness that we achieve can be very useful.

Truth can appear as lies.
Straightness can appear as twisted.
Skillfulness can appear to be clumsy.
Eloquence can sound like foolishness.

But the dialectic of yin and yang is not illusory.
Activity can overcome cold.
Tranquility can overcome heat.
And peacefulness is the natural seed of a violent world.

大成若缺其用不敝大盈若沖其用不窮大
直若屈大巧若拙大辯若訥躁勝寒靜勝
熱清靜為天下正

46
Enough Is Enough!

When the Great Integrity permeated our lives,
freely galloping horses fertilized the fields.

When the Great Integrity was lost,
war horses were bred in the countryside.

There is no greater calamity
than acquisitiveness racing out of control.

Only those who know when enough is enough
can ever have enough.

天下有道却走馬以糞天下無道戎馬生於郊罪莫大於可欲禍莫大於不知足咎莫大於欲得故知足之足常足矣

47

Going Beyond

We can understand the world as it is
without leaving our home.
We can understand the world as it might be
without peering dreamily out our window.

The further we go,
the less we know.

Wise people understand the 10,000 things
without going to each one.
They know them without having to look at each one,
and they transform all without acting on each one.

不出戶知天下不窺牖見天道其出彌遠其
知彌少是以聖人不行而知不見而名無為而
成

48

All Is Done Without Doing

To obtain a diploma requires the storage of trivia.
To obtain the Great Integrity requires their abandonment.

The more we are released from vested fragments of knowledge,
the less we are compelled to take vested actions,
until all is done without doing.

When the ego interferes
in the rhythms of process,
there is so much doing!
But nothing is done.

其有事不足以取天下

無為而無不為矣故取天下者常以無事及

為學日益為道日損損之又損以至於無為

49

Wisdom

Wise people are not absorbed
in their own needs.
They take the needs of all people as their own.

They are good to the good.
But they are also good to those
who are still absorbed in their own needs.

Why?
Because goodness is in the very nature
of the Great Integrity.

Wise people trust
those who trust.
But they also trust those who do not trust.

Why?
Because trusting is in the very nature
of the Great Integrity.

Wise people merge with all others
rather than stand apart judgmentally.
In this way, all begin to open their ears and hearts,
more prepared to return to the innocence of childhood.

聖人無常心以百姓心為心善者吾善之不善
者吾亦善之德善矣信者吾信之不信者吾
亦信之德信矣聖人之在天下惵惵為天下
渾其心百姓皆注其耳目聖人皆孩之

50

The Forces of Life and Death

Every one of us is born,
And everyone dies.

However, three of every ten
seem to be born to live,
three seem to be born to die,
and three live lifefully or deathfully
according to their chosen life styles.

But only one in ten
seems to survive all dangers.
When walking through the jungle,
she never fears the rhinoceros
because there seems to be no place in her to butt
    his horns.
She never fears the tiger
because there seems to be no place to sink his claws,
and she never fears weapons
because there seems to be no place their steel
    can penetrate.

This is the fulfilled person of the Great Integrity
who leaves no space in life for premature death.

出生入死生之徒十有三死之徒十有三人之

生動之死地亦十有三夫何故以其生生之厚

蓋聞善攝生者陸行不遇兕虎入軍不被

甲兵兕無所投其角虎無所措其爪兵無所

51

Natural Birthing

All in the universe derive from the Primal Integrity.
The interaction of yin and yang shapes and nourishes them,
and evolution ever transforms them
in their endless ecological dance.

Therefore, in its own way,
every entity celebrates its Primal Mother.
Not out of any mandate.
Not out of any obligation.
But solely as the expression of its own integrity.

容其刃夫何故以其無死地道生之德畜之

物形之勢成之是以萬物莫不尊道而貴

德道之尊德之貴夫莫之爵而常自然

故道生之畜之長之育之成之熟之養之

覆之生而不有為而不恃長而不宰是謂

玄德

天下有始以為天下母既得其母以知其子既知其子復守其母沒身不殆塞其兌閉其門終身不勤開其兌濟其事終身不救見小曰明守柔曰強用其光復歸其明無遺身殃是謂襲常

52

Returning to Our Origins

Everything has a common origin
that we might call the Mother of the Universe.

Once in pre-conscious times, we were all a part of this Mother,
just as we – all her children – were part of each other.

This was when we were all umbilically still attached
to the Great Integrity.

Some thousands of years ago, our species alone
issued a declaration of independence from our Mother.
Now it is time to reunite with her.

Thereafter, we will never any more suffer the 10,000 miseries
that only we human beings have acquired.

Block all the loopholes! Shut all the doors to the old temptations!
And we will never again feel deprived.

If we crawl through the loopholes, if we race through the gate
back to the 10,000 addictions, we will never be fulfilled.

How shall we know the Great Integrity?
When our insights proliferate even in the smallest matters.
When our strength is boundless even while ever yielding.

We can keep our outsights when returning to our insights.
In this way, we will reharmonize with our Mother,
celebrating the Great Integrity on a higher level.

53

Not Yet on the Way

Those who have the smallest grain of wisdom
would want to walk the simple path of the Great Integrity.
Their only fear would be to go astray.

Indeed, there is a good reason to fear
when most of the world is piled into two wagons
racing toward each other on a single-lane road.

In one overcrowded wagon is the vast majority
who live in weedy fields
with empty granaries.

In the other wagon are those
whose garments are opulently embroidered.
They gorge themselves
on rich foods far beyond their appetites,
and guzzle their inebriating drinks far beyond their thirst.

They accumulate wealth
even beyond their avaricious cravings
while armed to the teeth against their starving neighbors.

Surely such thievish degradation
couldn't be the way to the Great Integration.

非道也哉
彩帶利劍厭飲食資財有餘是謂盜夸
夷而民好徑朝甚除田甚蕪倉甚虛服父
使我介然有知行於大道唯施是畏大道甚夷

善建者不拔善抱者不脫子孫祭祀不輟脩之
身其德乃真脩之家其德乃餘脩之鄉其德乃
長脩之國其德乃豐脩之天下其德乃普故
以身觀身以家觀家以鄉觀鄉以國觀國以
天下觀天下吾何以知天下之然哉以此

54

The Whole Is in Each Part

Whatever is planted deeply is not easily uprooted.
Whatever is embraced sincerely does not crave escape.
Ever since we lost our intuition as our main guide in life,
these virtues have had to be consciously cultivated to survive.

Cultivate them in yourself and they will be genuine.
Cultivate them in your family and they will surely flourish.
Cultivate them in your community and they will be long-lasting.
Cultivate them in your country and they will be widely propagated.
Cultivate them in the world and they will certainly become universal.

In this way you will know others by what you do yourself.
You will know families by what you contribute as a family.
You will know the world by what you do as a planetary citizen.

How do we know all this?
Because we know that each part is the whole,
and the whole is in each part.

55

The Promises of the Great Integrity

舍德之厚比於赤子毒蟲不螫猛獸不據攫

鳥不搏骨弱筋柔而握固未知牝牡之合而朘

作精之至也終日號而嗌不嗄和之至也知和曰常

知常曰明益生曰祥心使氣曰強物壯則老是

謂不道不道早已

When we will live in complete integrity,
we will be innocent like newborn babies.
Wasps and scorpions will not sting us.
Wild beasts will not maul us.
Birds of prey will not seize us.

Our bones will be pliable, our sinews soft.
Yet our grip will be firm.
Even before we have known conjugality,
our sexuality will be easily aroused
because we will be so virile.

We'll sing all day long without becoming hoarse,
because we'll be in full harmony.
To be in harmony
is to live in the Great Integrity.
To live in the Great Integrity is the ultimate wisdom.

However, to interfere with nature is to seek control.
To seek control is to create dis-stress.
To create dis-stress produces exhaustion.
All these negations of the Great Integrity
also negate life and its longevity.

56
How to Prepare for the Great Integrity

Those who know don't lecture.
Those who lecture don't know.

To prepare the way for the Great Integrity –
Close the rationalizing routes!
Shut the gloomy gates!
Blunt the sharp edges!
Release those who are tethered!
Soften the blinding lights!
Unite the world!

We cannot achieve the Great Integrity
through intimacy or emotional detachment,
nor through posturing or humility.

Since the Great Integrity makes no judgments or demands,
how will we know when it has arrived?
When it permeates us with its universal "is-ness".

知者不言言者不知塞其兌開其門挫其銳解
其紛和其光同其塵是謂玄同不可得而親不
可得而疎不可得而利不可得而害不可得而
貴故為天下貴

57

Simplicity Blossoms When Coercion Dies

Govern a state with predictable actions.
Fight a war with surprise attacks.
But the universe becomes ours
only by eliminating coercive acts.
By not doing, nothing lacks.

How do we know these lessons?
By tuning into our Essence.

The more taboos and prohibitions
    there are,
the poorer the people become.
The more deadly weapons there are,
the more our fears turn us numb.

When craftiness spreads far,
the more bizarre what is done.
The stricter the laws there are,
the less the robbers run.

Therefore, the wise know
to make no one a foe.
The less coercing we do,
the more tranquilities grow.

When harmony reigns,
and we rule ourselves with felicity,
everyone gains,
and we'll all live in simplicity.

58
Alternatives

When a government is more benign,
the people are more productive.
When a government is more tyrannical,
the people are more rebellious.

But whatever the government,
if disaster is the bitter fruit of others' good fortune,
how long can such injustice be tolerated?
How long we have endured the hypocrisies!

Those pretending to be righteous act deceitfully.
Those pretending to be religious revert to evil.
We have been deluded!
And each day it becomes worse!

Be firm and armed, but do no harm!
Be as sharp as a knife, but do not cut!
Be ready to transform, but do not provoke!
Illuminate the darkness of ignorance, but do not blind!

其政悶悶其民淳淳其政察察其民缺缺禍
兮福所倚福兮禍所伏孰知其極其無正邪
正復為奇善復為妖民之迷其日固已久矣是以
聖人方而不割廉而不劌直而不肆光而不耀

59

The Importance of Moderation

To serve humanity,
there is nothing more important
than to be moderate.

To be moderate
is to return to the female yin principle.

To return to the yin
is to become nurturing.

To be nurturing
is to acquire enormous capacity.

To have enormous capacity
is to be ready for the Great Integrity

To be ready for the Great Integrity
is to be ready to serve humanity.

In this way we will become firmly planted
in the Great Integrity,
the pathway to a clear vision and a long life.

治人事天莫如嗇夫是謂早復早復謂之重積
德重積德則無不克無不克則莫知其極莫
知其極可以有國之毋可以長久是謂深根
固蔕長塋久視之道

60
Our Future

Govern a country like you would fry a small fish –
with care, respect and with the least interference.

When the world is governed according to the Great Integrity,
evil will lose its power.

Not only will evil lose its power,
it will no longer even exist.

When evil ceases to exist,
neither will good exist.

Without good and evil,
we simply will live totally in our human natures.

No one will compromise anyone else,
because we will all be inextricable parts of the Great Integrity.

治大國以烹小鮮以道蒞天下者其鬼不神
非其鬼不神其神不傷人聖人亦不傷人夫
兩不相傷故德交歸焉

61

A Plea For Mutual Humility

In our era,
when the Great Integrity has been lost,
separate states have arisen.
Some become very large.
Others remain very small.

When the larger ones
try to conquer the small,
at first the smaller ones are defeated
even though yang aggression
meets yang resistance.
But death stalks the people
on both sides of war.

Is it not better for great countries
to be like vast low lying lands
into which all streams passively go?

And the smaller countries,
like the innocent streams,
can be welcomed
at the end of their passage
by wide open arms,
calmly receiving their flow?

Would not this mutual humility
save countless lives now,
while serving as a rehearsal
for the coming of the Tao?

得其所欲故大者宜為下

不過過欲無畜人小國不過欲入事人兩者各

下大國則取大國故或下而取大國

牡以靜為下故大國以下小國則取小國小國以

大國者下流天下之交天下之交牝常以靜勝

Rehearsals for the Great Integrity

The Great Integrity is the sanctuary
of all human beings.

For those who are honest and caring,
it is a guide and a treasure.

For those who are dishonest and deceitful,
it is also a treasure,
because a good word can rationalize a selfish act,
and because a good act, now and then,
can serve as a mask for living extravagantly
from the misery of others.

Since the Great Integrity is so universally acknowledged,
don't cast away those who use it opportunistically.
Rather cast away the opportunities to live selfishly
so that the Great Integrity
can more fully permeate all our lives.

We might begin
with the inauguration ceremonies of our leaders.
Instead of showering them with precious gifts,
instead of the public swearing of meaningless oaths,
why not share a meditation on the Great Integrity
as a prelude to its comprehensive embrace?

道者萬物之奧善人之寶不善人之所保美言

可以市尊行可以加人人之不善何棄之有故

立天子置三公雖有拱璧以先駟馬不如坐進

此道古之所以貴此道者何也不曰求以得有

罪以免耶故為天下貴

63

The Secrets of Getting Things Done

Act without acting on.
Work without working at.

Enter bountifulness when it is still insufficiency.
Answer with kindness when faced with hostility.

Begin a difficult task in its easy stage,
because large problems grow from small ones.

Begin a large task in its formative state
because complex issues originate from
    simple ones.

But beware of those who promise quick and
    easy solutions!
Accept problems as challenges.

In this way, the sage accomplishes great tasks
without ever having to struggle with them.

難是以聖人由難之故終無難矣
圖難於其易為大於其細天下之難事必
作於易天下之大事必作於細是以聖人終不
為大故能成其大夫輕諾必寡信多易多
為無為事無事味無味大小多少報怨以德

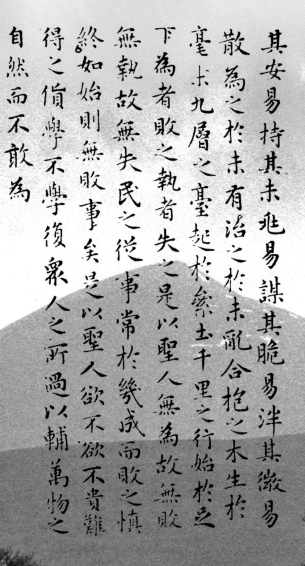

其安易持其未兆易謀其脆易泮其微易
散為之於未有治之於未亂合抱之木生於
毫末九層之臺起於累土千里之行始於足
下為者敗之執者失之是以聖人無為故無敗
無執故無失民之從事常於幾成而敗之慎
終如始則無敗事矣是以聖人欲不欲不貴難
得之貨學不學復眾人之所過以輔萬物之
自然而不敢為

It is easy to hold
what is still stable.
It is easy to mold
what is not yet formed.

It is easy to shatter
what is still fragile.
It is easy to scatter
what is yet light and small.

Therefore, act now rather than wait.
Get things done before it's too late.

A huge tree that you can't get your arms around
grows from a tiny seedling birth.
A tower of nine stories high
rises from a small heap of earth.

A thousand mile journey begins with one step.
This is an ancient tale.
Those who procrastinate
and those who take premature actions fail.

Those who interfere in processes disrupt them.
Those who hold tightly to possessions lose everything.
Wise people succeed because they never force an outcome.
They never suffer a loss, because they are not attached to anything.

Many succeed in gathering a few assets.
But when the stakes begin to sail, and
greed crashes through all cautionary boundaries,
failures unmercifully prevail.

Wise people don't accumulate possessions,
or teach anyone to amass things.
They devote themselves to the natural rhythms
that the Great Integrity brings.

65

The Loss of Innocence

In ancient times,
before there were those who were governed,
and those who governed over,
the sage blended with others,
and all was done through the Primal Simplicity.
People lived in innocence.

When the Great Fragmentation
replaced the Great Integrity,
cleverness defeated wisdom.
Even some enlightened sages
became victims of the rulers
commanding the highest intrigue.

古之善為道者非以明民將以愚之民之難治
以其智多故以智治國國之賊不以智治國國
之福知此兩者亦楷式能知楷式是謂玄德玄
德深矣遠矣與物反矣然後乃至大順

江海所以能為百谷王者以其善下之也故能為
百谷王是以聖人欲上人以其言下之欲先人以
其身下之是以聖人處上而人不重處前而人不
害是以天下樂推而不厭以其不爭故天下莫
能與之爭

66
Wisdom Always Comes from Below

Why do all the hundreds of great rivers
flow naturally to the sea?
Because the sea is always lower than the rivers.

When are thousands of people attracted to a sage?
When she positions herself below them,
always listening, tirelessly responding to their needs.

Never commanding.
Never coercing.
Never manipulating.

Such a sage is forever adored.
Since she treats everyone with love and respect,
everyone loves and respects her.

67

The Three Treasures

When most people hear about the Great Integrity, they say it is useless folly.
Because it is not like anything in the world we know, they also find it inconceivable.

On the contrary!
The Great Integrity has given us three treasures to cherish:
The first is love.
The second is moderation.
The third is humility.

If you love, you will be fearless.
If you are moderate, you might always sense abundance in life.
If you live in humility, you will be widely trusted.

But you will not have the capacity to love if you are fearful.
Even worse, if you are fearless and without love, you will always be courting disaster.

If you live in insufficiency, you have no opportunity to be moderate.
If you live in overabundance, you not only live immoderately,
but are always courting disaster.

If no one trusts you, then compensatory ego will preclude humility.
If everyone trusts you, and you lack humility, you will always court disaster.

The three treasures are practical guides to the Great Integrity.
The greatest foolishness is to live without them.

天下皆謂我道大似不肖夫惟大故似不肖
若肖久矣其細矣夫我有三寶保而持之一曰慈
二曰儉三曰不敢為天下先故能勇儉故
能廣不敢為天下先故能成器長今捨其
慈且勇捨其儉且廣捨其後且先死矣夫慈
以戰則勝以守則固天將救之以慈衛之

68

The Ethics of War

The best soldier fights
without vengeance,
without anger
and without hate.

He puts himself humbly
below his comrades,
thereby eliciting
the highest loyalty from them.

This is the power
of non-belligerence
and cooperation.
It is the ancient path to the Great Integrity.

力是謂配天古之極
善用人者為下是謂不爭之德是謂用人之
善為士者不武善戰者不怒善勝敵者不爭

69

In War the Defender Will Be Victorious

There is a saying
among those wise in military affairs:
"We do not act as host taking the initiative,
but would rather be the guest
assuming the defensive posture.
Rather than advancing one inch,
we would rather retreat one foot."

This is called
advancing without moving,
rolling up one's sleeves without baring one's arms,
fighting without weapons,
capturing the enemy without attacking.

There is no greater disaster
than boasting of one's invincibility.
Such boasts lead to the loss of the Three Treasures.
Therefore, when two opposing sides
meet in battle,
the one without an enemy
will be victorious.

加哀者勝矣

退尺是謂行無行攘無臂仍無敵執無兵

禍莫大於輕敵輕敵者幾喪吾寶故抗兵

用兵有言吾不敢為主而為客不敢進寸而

70
So Easy to Understand
and Practice!

The Great Integrity is so easy to understand,
and so easy to practice.
Yet it is not understood.
Nor is it practiced.

It is not understood
because people's heads are filled
with 10,000 trivia and rationalizations,
leaving no space for anything else.

It is not practiced
because people are kept busy, though bored,
with the 10,000 corruptions and miseries
that leave no time for the Three Treasures.

The Great Integrity is so ancient,
as old as the universe itself!
How can we expect people to remember it
after so many millennia of repression?

That is why
sages dress in rags
while they wear the Three Treasures
deep inside their hearts.

我者希則我貴矣是以聖人被褐懷玉

言有宗事有君夫惟無知是以不我知也知

吾言甚易知甚易行天下莫能知莫能行

知不知上不知知病夫惟病病是以不病
人不病以其病病是以不病聖

71
Healing the Mind

Academia confuses knowledge with knowing.
Most everyone applauds the memorization of the 10,000 trivia.
Beware! These schooled addictions are not just myths –
They are a form of mental illness.

Any fragment of the mind,
divorced from heart, spirit, human community,
and from the primal reality of the universe,
is an abomination of the Great Integrity.

Let us prepare for the Great Integrity
by cleansing ourselves of all these cobwebs
of cluttered fragments that paralyze the mind.
In this way we will function as our own holistic physicians.

72

Comparing Coercive Power and the Empowerment of the Great Integrity

When people no longer fear the power of governments,
a far greater empowerment appears –
the Great Integrity –
which never needs to enforce itself.

Then, we will never again be driven from our homes
or be compelled to labor for the benefit of others.
We will all work naturally to fulfill ourselves,
and to meet our community needs.

In the Great Integrity,
we will all love ourselves and all others,
not as compensations for ego deprivations and defilements,
but as natural expressions of our humanity.

見自愛不自貴故去彼取此

所生夫惟不厭是以不厭是以聖人自知不自

民不畏威而大威至矣無狎其所居無厭其

73

Courage, Patience and Paradoxes

The world we live in
requires great courage and patience.

Those with great courage, but little patience,
tend to kill or be killed.

Those with great courage as well as great patience
will tend to survive.

But the Great Integrity never judges you
for whatever path you happen to take.

The Great Integrity never strives
but always fulfills itself,

Never is commanded
but always responds.

Never is summoned
but always appears.

Never is impatient
but all is done on time.

勇於敢則殺勇於不敢則活此兩者或利或

害天之所惡孰知其故是以聖人猶難之天之

道不爭而善勝不言而善應不召而自來

繟然而善謀天網恢恢疏而不失

74
Ruling by Fear

People do not fear death
when they are forced to live in hopeless misery,
Thereby the executioners are no threat
to fearless rebels who dare to make trouble.
They might even execute the executioners.

When people do fear death,
they do not defy the executioners at first.
But how long can the killings go on
before those who fear death
also become fearless?
Then, they too might execute the executioners.

By that time, the only ones left
who might serve as the executioners
would be the people themselves.
However, it is said that those who hew wood
in place of skilled carpenters
are likely to cut their own hands.

希有不傷其手矣
而代司殺者殺是謂代大匠斲夫代大匠斲
而為奇者吾得執而殺之孰敢常有司殺者殺
民常不畏死奈何以死懼之若使民常畏死

75

Who Can Enjoy the Treasures of Life?

Why are the people so hungry?
Because their grain is devoured
by the rich in taxes.
That's why the people are starving.

Why are the people so rebellious?
Because the government deprives them
of their liberties and rights.
That's why the people are rebellious.

Why do the people not fear death?
Because their lives
are made so miserable
that death seems no worse than life.

Thus, no one can enjoy the treasures of life –
neither the rich who squander their humanity,
nor the government which tyrannizes the people,
nor the people who have nothing to gain from life.

民之飢以其上食稅之多是以飢民之難治以其
上之有為是以難治民之輕死以其上求生之厚
是以輕死夫惟無以生為者是賢於貴生

76

Let Yin Predominate Over Yang

When we are born,
we are soft and supple.
But when we've perished
there's no more tenderness
to be cherished.

When plants are young,
they are pliant and fragile.
When they die,
as they lose their green,
they wither and dry.

The sharp sword and knife
tryst always with death,
while love without strife
is an ever devoted
disciple of life.

An inflexible army
seals its own fate.
When a tree branch grows brittle,
it easily snaps,
whether long or little.

Wherever you go,
the rigid lie low.
While the weightless in the sky,
and all that is gentle,
fly boundlessly high.

人之生也柔弱其死也堅強草木之生也柔脆

其死也枯槁故堅強者死之徒柔弱者生之徒

是以兵強則不滕木強則共堅強處下柔弱

處上

77

Two Opposite Processes

The Way of the Great Integrity
is like stringing a bow,
pulling down the high,
lifting up the low –

Shortening the long,
lengthening the short
to take from the excessive
and give insufficiency support.

How opposite to our social norms
which increasingly impoverish the poor
to further enrich the rich
who do not need any more.

How can we gather the world's wealth
to create abundance for all in need?
Through rediscovering the Great Integrity,
by acting without praising the deed.

為而不恃功成不處其不欲見賢耶
有餘以奉不足於天下唯有道者是以聖人
足人之道則不然損不足以奉有餘孰能損
餘者損之不足者補之天之道損有餘而補不
天之道其猶張弓乎高者抑之下者舉之有

78

Appearance and Reality

天下莫柔弱於水而攻堅強者莫之能勝以其
無以易之故柔勝剛弱勝強天下莫不知而莫
能行是以聖人云受國之垢是謂社稷主受國
不祥是謂天下王正言若反

Nothing in the world
is softer and weaker than water.
Yet there is nothing better
for subduing all that is harder and stronger.

Everyone observes how weak overcomes strong,
how gentleness overcomes rigidity.
Yet this principle is seldom put into conscious practice.

Though some may say it is useless
to accept responsibility
for the calamities and toxicities of the world,
taking such responsibility
might put us on the road to the Great Integrity.

Just remember that truth often masquerades as falsity,
and falsity as truth.

79

The Toxicity of Blame

Harboring a resentment
is sure to leave some resentment behind.
How can this be good?
It cannot.
Therefore, the wise accept all responsibility.

Although those who hold the power
keep blaming and bleeding the people,
the violated Great Integrity blames no one.
Once achieving the Great Integrity,
we will all function with a pure heart.

和大怨必有餘怨安可以為善是以聖人執左
契而不責於人故有德司契無德司徹天道
無親常與善人

80

Transforming Our Lives

小國寡民使民有什伯之器而不用使民重死
而不遠徙雖有舟車無所乘之雖有甲兵無
所陳之使民復結繩而用之甘其食美其服
安其居樂其俗鄰國相望雞犬之聲相聞
民至老死不相往來

Let us fashion small states with few inhabitants
who, without stress,
can produce more than they require,
who are so happy with their lives
that they have no thought of migrating elsewhere –

Who inherit weapons and armor,
but no need to use them,
who return to honest forms of communication,
and the simple enjoyments
of an ecological way of life.

Although these states may be so close to each other
that they hear the barking of each other's dogs
and the crowing of each other's cocks,
living contentedly,
they will have no need to invade each other's space.

81

The Paradoxes of Life

信言不美美言不信善者不辯辯者不善
知者不博博者不知聖人無積既以為人己愈
既以與人己愈多天之道利而不害人之道

Profound words are not clever.
Clever words are not profound.

Wise people are not quarrelsome.
Quarrelsome people are not wise.

Those who are intelligent are not ideologues.
Those who are ideologues are not intelligent.

The enlightened never hoard anything.
They share their possessions.

The more they give,
the greater their abundance.

The Great Integrity is the physician of the universe
who heals without harming and who acts without contention.

SELECTED ENGLISH EDITIONS

Blakney, R.B.: *The Way of Life: Tao Te Ching by Lao Tzu*. Penguin, New York, 1955/83.

Bynner, Witter: *The Way of Life According to Lao Tzu: An American Version*. Capricorn Books, New York, 1944.

Carus, Paul: *The Teachings of Lao-Tzu: The Tao Te Ching*. St. Martin's Press, New York, 1913/2000.

Chan, Alan K.L.: *Two Visions of the Way: A Study of the Wang Pi and Ho-shang Kung Commentaries on the Lao Tzu*. State University of New York Press, Albany, NY, 1991.

Chen, Ellen M.: *The Tao Te Ching: A New Translation with Commentary*. Paragon House, New York, 1989.

Cheng, Man-jan: *Lectures on the Tao Teh Ching: My Words Are Very Easy To Understand* (trans. T.C. Gibbs) (translation and commentary). North Atlantic Books, Richmond, CA, 1981.

Dalton, Jerry O.: *Backward Down the Path: A New Approach to the Tao Te Ching*. Humanics Publishing Group, Atlanta, Georgia, 1994/1998.

Degen, Richard: *Tao Te Ching for the West*. Hohm Press, Prescott, Arizona, 1999.

Feng Gia-Fu, and English, Jane: *Lao Tsu – Tao Te Ching*. Random House, New York, 1972, Vintage Books, 1997.

Freke, Timothy: *Lao Tzu's Tao Te Ching*. Piatkus Books, London, 1995/1999.

Grigg, Ray: *The New Lao Tzu: A Contemporary Tao Te Ching*. Charles E. Tuttle, Boston, 1995.

Henricks, Robert G.: *Lao-Tzu Te-Tao Ching: A New Translation Based on the Recently Discovered Ma-Wang-Tui Texts*. Ballantine Books, New York, 1992/1999.

Hinton, David: *Tao Te Ching: Lao Tzu*. Counterpoint Press, Washington, DC, 2000.

Hwang, Shi Fu: *Tao Teh Ching: The Taoist's New Library*. Taoism Publishers, Austin, Texas, 1987/1991.

LaFargue, Michael: *The Tao of the Tao Te Ching: A Translation and Commentary*. State University of New York Publishers, Albany, New York, 1992.

Lau, D.C.: *Lao Tzu – Tao Te Ching*. Penguin, London, 1964.

Mair, Victor H.: *Tao Te Ching: The Classic Book of Integrity and the Way Based on the Recently Discovered Ma-Wang-Tui Manuscripts*. Bantam Books, London, 1990.

Miles, Thomas H.: *Tao Te Ching – Lao Tzu: About the Way of Nature and its Powers*. Avery, Garden City Park, NY, 1992.

Mitchell, Stephen: *Tao Te Ching*. Harper & Row, New York, London, 1988/1992.

Ni, Hua-Ching: *Esoteric Tao Teh Ching*. College of Tao & Traditional Chinese Healing, Santa Monica, CA, 1992 and Sevenstar Communications Group, Santa Monica, CA, 1992.

Ni, Hua-Ching: *The Complete Works of Lao Tzu: Tao Teh Ching & Hua Hu Ching*. Sevenstar Communications Group, Santa Monica, CA, 1979/93.

Pine, Red: *Lao-Tzu's Taoteching: With Selected Commentaries of the Past 2000 Years*. Mercury House, San Francisco, 1996/2001.

Ren Jiyu: *A Taoist Classic: The Book of Lao Zi*. Foreign Languages Press, Beijing, 1991/1995.

Star, Jonathan: *Tao Te Ching: The Definitive Edition* (translation and commentary). Jeremy P. Tarcher/Putnam, New York, 2001.

Walker, Brian Browne: *The Tao Te Ching of Lao Tzu*. St. Martin's Press, New York, 1996.

Wilhelm, Richard: *Lao Tzu – Tao Te Ching: The Book of Meaning and Life*. Penguin, London, 1999.

Wu, John C.: *Tao Teh Ching*. Shambhala Publications, London, 1989/1990.

Yutang, Lin: *The Wisdom of Laotse* (translation and commentary). The Modern Library, New York, 1948/76.

VERBATIM TRANSLATIONS CONSULTED

Cheng, Yan: Manuscript 1996.

Johnson, Mark and Choo-Li, Chi: Manuscript 1997.

Richter, Gregory C.: *Gate of All Marvelous Things: A Guide to Reading the Tao Te Ching*. Red Mansions Publishing, South San Francisco, CA, 1998.

Star, Johathan: *Tao Te Ching: The Definitive Edition*. Jeremy P. Tarcher/Putnam, New York, 2001.

REFERENCES

Auricular Acupuncture Therapy. Compiled by the Zoological Research Institute of the Chinese Academy of Science, 1972/74. (In Chinese.)

Bahr, F.R.: *The Chinese Meridians in their Projections on the Auricle* (wall chart). F.R. Bahr, Munich, Germany, 1999.

Bateson, G.: *Mind and Nature, A Necessary Unity*. Bantam, New York, 1979.

Bohm, D.: *Wholeness and the Implicate Order*. Routledge and Kegan Paul, London, 1980.

Bohm, D., Weber R.: "The Enfolding-Unfolding Universe: A Conversation with David Bohm". In K. Wilber (ed) *The Holographic Paradigm and Other Paradoxes: Exploring the Leading Edge of Science*. Shambala, Boston, 1985.

Buck, R.M.: *Cosmic Consciousness: A Classic Investigation of the Development of Man's Mystic Relationship to the Infinite*. E.P. Dutton, New York, 1969.

Caldicott, H.: *If You Love This Planet: A Plan to Heal the Earth*. W.W. Norton, New York and London, 1992.

Capra, F.: *The Tao of Physics*. Shambhala, Boston, 1975/85.

: *The Turning Point*. Bantam, New York, 1982/88.

Chaisson, E.: *The Life Era: Cosmic Selection and Conscious Evolution*. W.W. Norton, New York, 1989.

De Chardin, T.: *The Future of Man*. HarperCollins, New York, 1959.

Csikszentmihalyi, M.: *The Evolving Self: A Psychology for the Third Millennium*. HarperCollins, New York, 1993.

Dale, A.: "The Future of Music: An Investigation into the Evolution of Forms". *The Journal of Aesthetics and Art Criticism*, XXVI/4, 1968 (1)

: "The Rise and Fall of the Scale: Toward a Social History of the Musical Scale".
Acta, International Congress of Aesthetics, Stockholm, 1968 (2)

: "The Micro-Meridians of the Ear and the Foot Acupuncture Systems" (with M.D.
Huang), *American Journal of Chinese Medicine*, Vol 2, Suppl. 1. Proceedings of the Third
World Symposium on Acupuncture and Chinese Medicine, 1975.

: "The Micro-Acupuncture Systems Part I". *American Journal of Acupuncture*, 1976; 4 (1): 7–24.

: "The Micro-Acupuncture Systems Part II". *American Journal of Acupuncture*, 1976; 4(3):
207–227.

: "The Origins and Future of Acupuncture". *American Journal of Acupuncture*, 1982;
10 (2): 101–120.

: "The Principles and Systems of Micro-Acupuncture". *International Journal of Chinese
Medicine*, 1984; 1(4): 15–42.

: "The Micro-Acupuncture Meridians". *International Journal of Chinese Medicine*, 1985;
2(2): 31–49.

: *Dictionary of Acupuncture: Terms, Concepts and Points*. Dialectic Publishing, N. Miami
Beach, FL, 1993.

: "An Outline Evolution of Consciousness, Medicine and Social Relations". *Alternative
Medicine Journal*, 1995; 2 (5): 18–26.

: "The Systems, Holograms and Theory of Micro-Acupuncture". *American Journal of
Acupuncture*, 1999; 27(3/4): 207–242.

Diamond, J.: *Guns, Germs, and Steel: The Fates of Human Societies*. W.W. Norton, New York,
London, 1997/99.

Dossey, L.: *Space, Time & Medicine*. Shambhala, Boulder and London, 1982.

Drexler, E. and Peterson, C. with Pergamit, C.: *Unbounding the Future: The Nanotechnology
Revolution*. William Morrow, New York, 1991.

Eisler, R.: *The Chalice and the Blade*. Harper, San Francisco, 1987.

Elgin, D.: *Awakening Earth: Exploring the Human Dimensions of Evolution*. William Morrow,
New York, 1993.

Ferguson, M.: *The Aquarian Conspiracy: Personal and Social Transformation in Our Time*.
Jeremy Tarcher/Putnam, New York, 1980/1987.

Frankl, V.: *Man's Search for Meaning*. Washington Square Press, New York, 1985.

Fuller, B.: *Operating Manuel for Space Ship Earth*. The Penguin Group, New York, 1991.

Gazzaniga, M.S.: "The Split Brain". In *Man and The Nature of Consciousness*, ed. R.E.
Ornstein, Viking Press, 1973, pp 87–100.

Greene, B.: *The Elegant Universe: Superstrings, Hidden Dimensions, and the Quest for the
Ultimate Theory*. W.W. Norton, New York and London, 1999.

Grof, S.: *The Adventure of Self-Discovery: Dimensions of Consciousness and New Perspectives in
Psychotherapy and Inner Exploration*. State University of New York Press, New York, 1988.

Grosso, M.: *The Millennium Myth: Love and Death at the End of Time*. Quest, Wheaton,
Illinois, 1995.

Hegel, G.W.: *The Philosophy of Hegel*. Ed. C.J. Friedrich. Modern Library, New York, 1953.

Henderson, H.: *Building a Win-Win World: Life Beyond Global Economics*. Barrett-Koehler, San Francisco, 1996.

Houston, J.: *Life-Force: The Psycho-Historical Recovery of the Self*. Delacorte, New York, 1980.

Hubbard, B.M.: *The Evolutionary Journey: A Personal Guide to a Positive Future*. Evolutionary Press, San Rafael, California, 1982.

: *Conscious Evolution: Awakening the Power of Our Social Potential*. New World Library, Novato, California, 1998.

Ivanov-Smolenksy, A.G.: *Essays on the Pathophysiology of the Higher Nervous System*, Foreign Languages Publishing House, English ed., 1954. (Original Russian ed. 1949/52.)

Jantsch, E.: *Design of Evolution: Self-Organization and Planning in the Life of Human Systems*. George Braziller, New York, 1975.

Laszlo, E.: *Evolution: The Grand Synthesis*. Shambhala, Boston and London, 1987.

Leonard, G.B.: *The Transformation: A Guide to the Inevitable Changes in Humankind*. Delacorte Press, New York, 1972.

Lerner, E.J.: *The Big Bang Never Happened*. Vintage Books, Random House, New York, 1991/92.

Maslow, A.H.: *The Further Reaches of Human Nature*. Penguin, New York, 1993.

McLaughlin, C. and Davidson, G.: *Spiritual Politics: Changing the World from the Inside Out*. Ballantine Books, New York, 1994.

Murphy, M.: *The Future of the Body: Explorations into the Further Evolution of Human Nature*. Jeremy P. Tarcher, Los Angeles, 1992.

Needham, J. and Lu, G.D.: *Celestial Lancets: A History & Rationale of Acupuncture & Moxa*. Cambridge University Press, Cambridge, England, 1980.

Needham, J. and Ronan, C.A.: *The Shorter Science & Civilization in China*. Cambridge University Press, Cambridge, 1978.

Ornstein, R.F.: *Multimind*. Houghton Mifflin, Boston, 1986.

: *The Right Mind: Making Sense of the Hemispheres*. Harcourt Brace, New York, 1997.

Pavlov, I.P.: *Twenty Years of Objective Study of the Higher Nervous System Activity in Animals*, State Medical and Biological Publishing House, 1938.

Peck, M.S.: *The Road Less Traveled and Beyond: Spiritual Growth in an Age of Anxiety*. Simon & Schuster, New York, 1997.

Piaget, J.: *The Origin of Intelligence in Children* (trans. M Cook). WW Norton, 1963.

: *The Grasp of Consciousness* (trans. S Wedgewood). Harvard Univ. Press, 1976.

Polak, F.: *The Image of the Future: The 21st Century and Beyond*. Prometheus Books, Buffalo, NY, 1976.

Pribram, K.H.: "Toward a Holonomic Theory of Perception". In Ertel, S. (ed.) *Gestalttheorie in der Modernen Psychologie*. Steinkopff, Darmstadt, Germany, 1975.

: *Languages of the Brain: Experimental Paradoxes and Principles in Neuropsychology*. Brandon House, New York, 1982 and Erlbaull Assoc., Hillsdaly, NJ, 1990.

Rajneesh, B.S.: *Tao – The Three Treasures: Talks on Fragments from Tao Te Ching by Lao Tzu, Vol. I*. Rajneesh Foundation International, Rajneeshpuram, Oregon, 1976.

: *Tao – The Three Treasures: Talks on Tao Tzu. Vol. 4.* Rajneesh Foundation, Poona, India, 1977.

: *The Way of Tao: Discourse on Lao Tse's Tao-Te Ching, Vol I* (trans. Dolli Didi). Motilal Banarsidass, Delhi, India, 1978.

: *The Way of Tao: Discourse on Lao Tse's Tao-Te Ching, Vol II* (trans. Dolli Didi). Motilal Banarsidass, Delhi, India, 1979.

: *The New Man: The Only Hope for the Future.* Rebel Publ House GmbH, Cologne, Germany, 1987.

Reich, W.: *Listen, Little Man!* (trans. R. Manheim. Illus. W. Steil). Farrar, Straus and Giroux, New York, 1948.

: *People in Trouble: The Emotional Plague of Mankind* (trans. P. Schmitz). Farrar, Straus and Giroux, New York, 1953.

Roszak, T.B.: *The Voice of the Earth.* Simon & Schuster, New York, 1992.

Russell, P.: *The Global Brain Awakens: Our Next Evolutionary Leap.* Global Brain, Palo Alto, CA, 1995.

Sagan, C.: *Billions & Billions: Thoughts on Life and Death at the Brink of the Millennium.* Ballantine, New York,1997.

Sahtouris, E.: *Gaia – The Human Journey from Chaos to Cosmos.* Pocket Books, New York and London, 1989.

: *Earth Dance: Living Systems in Evolution.* Metalog Books, Alameda, CA, 1995.

Salk, J.: *Anatomy of Reality: Merging of Institution and Reason.* Columbia University Press, New York, 1983.

Sheldrake, R.: *A New Science of Life: The Hypothesis of Formative Causation.* J.P. Tarcher, Los Angeles, 1981.

Shlain, L.: *The Alphabet Versus the Goddess: The Conflict Between Word and Image.* Penguin, Middlesex, England/New York, 1998/99.

Sivik, T. and Schoenfeld, R.: "Somatization and the Paradigm of Psychosomatology". *Advances in Mind – Body Medicine* 2001; 17: 263–266.

Stock, G.: *Metaman: The Merging of Humans and Machines into a Global Superorganism.* Simon and Schuster, New York, 1993.

Talbot, M.: *The Holographic Universe.* HarperPerennial, New York, 1991.

Vygotsky, L.S.: *Thought and Language.* Ed. A. Kozulin. MIT Publ, Boston, 1986. (Original Russian edition, 1934.)

Wilber, K.: *The Holographic Paradigm and Other Paradoxes: Exploring the Leading Edge of Science.* Shambhala, Boston and London, 1985.

: *Sex, Ecology, Spirituality: The Spirit of Evolution.* Shambhala, Boston and London, 1995.

: *A Brief History of Everything.* Shambhala, Boston and London, 1996.

Williamson, M.: *A Return to Love.* HarperCollins, New York, 1996.

Yoo, T.W.: *Koryo Sooji Chim.* Eum Yang Maek Jin Publ., Seoul, Korea, 1977 (in Korean) and *Koryo Hand Acupuncture.* P. Eckman, ed. 1988 (in English).

Young, A.M.: *The Reflexive Universe: Evolution of Consciousness.* Delacorte, New York, 1976.

Zukav, G.: *The Seat of the Soul.* Simon & Schuster, New York, 1990.

NOTES

INTRODUCTION

1   There are two transliterations of Mandarin Chinese in current use: the older *Wade-Giles* and the more recent *Pinyin*. Although current publications generally utilize the Pinyin, most people are familiar with the Wade-Giles spelling of the tide (*Tao Te Ching*) and the presumed author of this book (*Lao Tzu*) rather than the Pinyin (*Dao De Jing* by *Lao Zi*). Therefore in this case, and in all others where readers may be familiar with a name or word in the Wade-Giles spelling, I use this. In all other cases, I use the Pinyin spelling, often also giving the Wade-Giles in parenthesis.

2   Needham, the foremost Western historian of the development of Chinese science from the earliest ancient times, proposes that Lao Tzu lived in the 4th century BCE (Needham-Ronan, 1978, p.87).

3   First stanza of Verse 1.

4   For an explicit reference to Tao as the greatness of all entities and of the universe, see Verse 25.

5   According to Cheng 1981, p.1.

6   See Schlain 1998.

7   From Verse 1.

8   Although purely non-confrontational modes may have been the best option for Lao Tzu's challenges to the establishment of his time, it is not to say that polemics and confrontational modes of action are not sometimes appropriate methods for us to facilitate change.

9   Our right cerebral hemisphere, according to psychophysiological findings of the past 25 years, functions as a more holistic consciousness, while the left hemisphere tends to be in charge of language-mediated rational (as well as rationalizing) thought. (See Gazzaniga 1973; Ornstein 1986; 1997; and Schlain 1998/99.) Pavlov referred to right-brain consciousness as our *First Signaling System* and to left-brain consciousness as our *Second Signaling System*. (See Pavlov 1938; and Ivanov-Smolensky 1954.) The physiological mediator and neurological "traffic director" for these two disparate functions is the corpus callosum, which connects the two cerebral hemispheres. It is important to understand the differentiation of left and right-brain functions because Lao Tzu, without knowing about our split brain, implies, throughout the *Tao Te Ching*, that we can only walk the path toward the Great Integrity by releasing ourselves from our rationalizing prisons (left brain) and allowing our intuition (right brain) to play a greater role.

10 *Yin and Yang* is the ancient Chinese terminology for the concept that everything in our universe expresses itself in polarities; that is, in two fundamental contradictory as well as balancing forces (for example, active and passive, positive and negative, hot and cold), which both oppose and complement each other. The theory of polarities developed during the time of Lao Tzu, specifically in the Spring and Autumn Period (770–476 BCE during the Zhou (Chou) dynasty) (Dale 1993, p.82 and pp.247–249).

11 See Schlain 1998.

12 Lao Tzu's five premises about the Great Integrity are: 1) It is the origin and nature of the universe to be integral – that is, for the whole to be contained in every part and for every part to be inextricable from the whole. Lao Tzu referred to this characterization of reality as the Tao – the Great Integrity. 2) In what Lao Tzu called "ancient times", human beings, just as every other species, lived in harmony with the Great Integrity. 3) All this changed for us human beings living in relatively recent "civilized" times when we became separated from nature and began relating to each other, and even to ourselves, as enemies to be conquered. This is attributable to the loss of the Great Integrity. It is the root of all the forms of misery that human beings experience. 4) Some day we will all return to the Great Integrity as the form and substance of all our lives. 5) The Great Integrity is not only an alternative way of life that we can realize some time in the future, but it is the very pathway to our transcendence. The implication is that it is a guide for our behavior and consciousness right now as we reinvest our institutions and ourselves.

13 From Verse 15. For Lao Tzu, "ancient times" was the long period of tribal life that preceded civilization, and also perhaps the first 1,000 years of Chinese civilization, the legendary period between 4,000 and 2,500 BCE.

14 How can we know how it feels to be in the Great Integrity? Paradoxically, one way of acquiring a concrete image of a *future* non-toxic life style is by observing the past; for example, by studying some tribal peoples before they become physically, mentally, emotionally and spiritually corrupted by civilization's uncivilized ways. A second way of acquiring a concrete image of a non-toxic life style is by observing the innocence of young children before they are corrupted.

15 From Rajneesh 1976, pp.272–273.

16 From Verse 2.

17 See Note 9.

18 The following authors are keen observers and activists of the transition to the Third Epoch and invite us to join them as conscious participants in the process: Bateson 1979; Bohrn/Weber 1985; Bohm 1980; Buck 1969; Caldicott 1992; Capra 1975/85; and 1982/88; Chaisson 1989; Csikszentmihalyi 1993; Dale 1968 (1 & 2); 1982; and 1995; Diamond 1997/99; Dossey 1982; Drexler et al 1991; Eisler 1987; Elgin 1993; Ferguson 1980/1987; Frankl 1985; Fuller 1991; Greene 1999; Grof 1988; Grosso 1995; Henderson 1996; Houston 1980; Hubbard 1982 and 1998; Jantsch 1975; Laszlo 1987; Leonard 1972; McLaughlin et al 1994; Murphy 1992; Feck 1997; Polak 1976; Rajneesh 1987; Roszak 1992; Sagan 1997; Sahtouris 1989; and 1995; Salk 1983; Sheldrake 1981; Stock 1993; Wilber 1995 and 1996; Williamson 1996; Young 1976 and Zukav 1990.

19 That is, what Lao Tzu called the Tao (the Great Integrity). For us, the emergence of an integral consciousness requires our transcendence of the mechanistic and atomistic premises of Newtonian–Cartesian science, as well as the philosophical and theological premises of dualism.

20 From Verse 7.

21 Cheng ms 1996.

22 Chi and Johnson ms 1997.

23 Richter 1998.

24 Star 2001.

25 See list of selected English editions.

INDEX OF VERSE TITLES

BOOKS BY RALPH ALAN DALE

Chinese Medicine

The Acupuncture Comprehensive Prescriptive Index

Dictionary of Acupuncture Terms, Concepts and Points

Acupuncture: The Special Function Points

Acupuncture with Your Fingers

The Macro-Acupuncture Manual

The Acupuncture Certification Review Book of Questions and Answers

Acupoint Exercises for the Six Senses

Music

Music in the Round

Accompanied Rounds

Rhythm: Activities and Instruments

Books for Children

When I Met Robin

Shoes, Pennies and Rockets

Lenore and the Wonder House

Games to Sing and Play

The Dale Recorder Method